HOW TO PASS

In full
COLOUR

HIGHER

HISTORY

SECOND EDITION

Sandy Burgess
Simon Wood

HODDER
GIBSON
AN HACHETTE UK COMPANY

Suggested approaches to answering the practice source questions in Chapter 11 are available at www.hoddereducation.co.uk/htphigherhistory.

The Publishers would like to thank the following for permission to reproduce copyright material:

Photo credits
Page 63 © Herald and Times Group; page 72 Library of Congress, Prints & Photographs Division, WW1 Posters, LC-USZC4-11046; running head image © Photodisc/Getty Images.

Acknowledgements
Extracts from Question Papers are reproduced by permission of the Scottish Qualifications Authority.

Every effort has been made to trace all copyright holders, but if any have been inadvertently overlooked the Publishers will be pleased to make the necessary arrangements at the first opportunity.

Although every effort has been made to ensure that website addresses are correct at time of going to press, Hodder Gibson cannot be held responsible for the content of any website mentioned in this book. It is sometimes possible to find a relocated web page by typing in the address of the home page for a website in the URL window of your browser.

Hachette UK's policy is to use papers that are natural, renewable and recyclable products and made from wood grown in sustainable forests. The logging and manufacturing processes are expected to conform to the environmental regulations of the country of origin.

Orders: please contact Bookpoint Ltd, 130 Milton Park, Abingdon, Oxon OX14 4SB. Telephone: (44) 01235 827720. Fax: (44) 01235 400454. Lines are open 9.00–5.00, Monday to Saturday, with a 24-hour message answering service. Visit our website at www.hoddereducation.co.uk. Hodder Gibson can be contacted direct on: Tel: 0141 848 1609; Fax: 0141 889 6315; email: hoddergibson@hodder.co.uk

Cover photo © Orlando Florin Rosu/Alamy
Illustrations by Peter Lubach at Redmoor Design
Typeset in 10.5 on 14pt Frutiger Light by Phoenix Photosetting, Chatham, Kent
Printed in Italy

A catalogue record for this title is available from the British Library

ISBN: 978 1444 11273 3

CONTENTS

INTRODUCTION

Welcome to this Revision Book!

You are clearly an intelligent student, as you have decided to study Higher History. This book aims to give you advice on the skills needed to complete and pass the Higher History course successfully. In studying History you are studying a subject of great importance that is enjoyable and interesting. Not only is History about you, your heritage and the past, but it is a subject which gives you skills that are attractive to employers and which make you a useful citizen.

◆ History teaches you how to work on your own initiative or with others.

◆ History teaches you to research, analyse and communicate your findings with others.

◆ History teaches you to defend and support your opinions against criticism.

◆ History is essential for learning the core skills of the workplace.

In this rapidly changing world employers want people who are

◆ independent thinkers

◆ open-minded

◆ disciplined

◆ good at problem solving

◆ able to pick out the important from the unimportant.

Higher History delivers these qualities.

The Higher History course is structured in the following way.

Element of assessment	Timing	Structure	Marks
Paper 1	Examination of 1 hour 20 minutes	2 essays	2 × 20-mark essays
		One on British History	
		One on European and World History	40 marks
Paper 2	Examination of 1 hour 25 minutes	Source-based paper on Scottish History	Questions will be worth 5, 5, 10 and 10 marks
		5 sources	
		4 questions	30 marks
Extended Essay	Supervised write-up of 2 hours	Independently researched essay on topic you choose	30 marks

This gives an overall total of 100 marks. This book will take you through each of the three elements of assessment. Good luck in your studies and, above all, enjoy the course that you are doing!

SECTION 1

Essay Questions

ANSWERING ESSAY QUESTIONS

In Paper 1 of the Higher History examination, you will have to write *two* essays, each of which is worth 20 marks. These two essays make up 40% of your total mark, so it is essential that your two essays are as good as you can possibly make them.

You may well find this prospect daunting and alarming. In History classes further down the school, you have undoubtedly written essay-type answers – perhaps reporting on research you have carried out. However, these were probably quite short – two or three paragraphs in length.

Now, suddenly, here you are tackling Higher History, and your teacher is expecting you to write big essays! … on important historical topics! … and you have got to get this right!

You could be forgiven for feeling a little apprehensive or nervous at what you are being asked to do. Well – don't worry! You can **learn** how to write a successful History essay. It's actually quite a straightforward process once you get started. **You will need to put in some solid work and effort** – but you already knew that when you signed up for Higher History.

A skill worth having?

Definitely! Learning how to write a Higher History essay – how to structure, organise and present your thoughts and opinions on a specific subject – is a really useful thing to do. It is a valuable skill to possess, and can be of immense usefulness to you in a wide range of careers. In addition, it is a skill which is supremely important if you are considering working at university level.

How long should a Higher History essay be?

Many candidates starting out on the Higher History course ask this question. The answer is a time-honoured one, and it might sound a bit smart:

How long have you got?

No, this is not an attempt to be smart, or to humiliate you. It is, in fact, a very important question – probably the central question to help you achieve success in Paper 1.

You have a maximum of 40 minutes for each essay.

In fact, you will probably have a bit less than this, as you will have to spend a few minutes looking at the paper, and deciding which two questions you want to do. By the time you have done that, your available time is probably down to around 36 or 37 minutes. This is the amount of time available to you as you work on the two essays which are required in Paper 1. In other words, time is at a premium in Paper 1! So it is very important that you do not waste any of it, and concentrate your efforts on your best possible work.

Concentration – the key to success in writing an essay!

You start with zero!

Well, obviously – you always start with zero. Before you have even put pen to paper, you have a mark of zero! However, it may help you get into the right mindset for essay writing if you think like this:

Zero out of twenty is the lowest possible mark which you can get.

Twenty out of twenty is the highest possible mark.

So, it may help you in your essay writing if you think like this:

How do I move my mark for this essay away from zero, and as close to twenty as possible?

Some positives to begin with

As you start to think about how to achieve success in writing Higher History essays, let's begin with some of the positives – with the fact that you already have a number of things going for you.

- ◆ You have chosen to do Higher History – so it probably follows from this that you have an interest in the subject.

- ◆ You will already be building up an increasingly detailed knowledge of the significant facts and events of the periods being studied in your course. You have used textbooks, class notes and handouts, history websites, possibly pieces of film, or DVDs. You are beginning to understand what was happening, what was going on.

- ◆ This knowledge is important. These are the information and details which you will use in your essay writing – the raw materials of your essay.

- ◆ Your first priority is, therefore, obvious – **know the facts**. Get this right from the outset! **Concentrate** on building up your knowledge. Don't harm your chances of success because of lack of knowledge, because you are confused about something, or because you have not understood something completely. Read over your notes – check with your colleagues – ask your teacher. But – **get the facts right**!

You know that you will have to write **two** essays and that they will be on subjects which you have studied in class. Your teacher will have made sure that you have covered the **course content** – the actual facts and information which you need to know in order to complete the two essays. You will probably have been given textbooks to study, worksheets and factsheets to plough through; you will probably have used some websites on the Internet, and looked at some material on video or DVD.

In other words, you **know** the basic facts of the periods which you have been studying! You will have studied:

◆ the principal characters or people involved

◆ the main changes and developments which took place

◆ the main reasons for the changes …

◆ and so on.

If you are studying Higher History, then one thing is certain – you will end up **knowing** a lot of stuff! To achieve success in Paper 1, with your two essays, this is **vital**. However, knowing your History will not be enough in itself to achieve success in Paper 1. There is more to achieving success in this paper than simply being able to remember lots of factual content and knowledge.

In a Higher History essay, you will also have to **think** and **make judgements** about the period you have studied, and the range of **issues** which have arisen during it. It is this process of **thinking** and **making judgements** which is central to your success in Paper 1. The better you become at this, the more marks you are likely to attain.

MY REFERENCE LIBRARY

Think of your own reference library, holding all the relevant knowledge and information you will need to write successful essays in Higher History:

◆ textbooks

◆ class notes

◆ factsheets/handouts

◆ worksheets

◆ videos/DVDs

◆ website information.

It is vital that you do two things:

◆ Make sure that there are no gaps in your knowledge.

◆ Make sure that you **read** and **review** your notes thoroughly. Ask your teacher for advice if there is anything that you do not understand.

What You Should Know

Knowing facts is not enough! In Higher History you need to be able to **think** about the facts and information – to show not just that you know them, but also that you **understand** them. You will have to show that you can:

◆ **analyse** relevant information

◆ **make judgements** about important historical developments and changes

◆ **evaluate** these developments and changes

◆ **consider** a variety of factors, and make an assessment of their relative importance.

Hints and Tips

Three very important letters:

A T Q

ANSWER THE QUESTION!

Answer the question … the question on the examination paper … focus very directly on that question – and nothing else!

Read the question.

Read it **again**.

◆   What is the question asking you to do?

◆   Have you understood it properly?

◆   Do you know what you are being asked to do? Are you sure?

◆   You can now make a start on attempting to **answer** it!

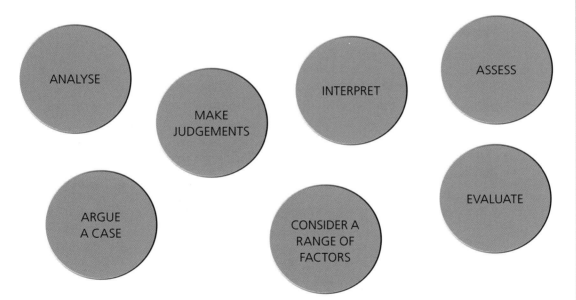

Feeling anxious that you might not be able to do all these things? Maybe even verging towards sheer blind panic? Chill out a little. You are already able to do most of these things, though you might not have been aware of it.

Let's think about football for a little while. Yes, that's right – **football**!

No, it's not as daft as it sounds. We are going to use football as an illustration, which may help you to understand about analysing, evaluating, making judgements and all the other heavy-duty skills you are going to need in Higher History.

Let's imagine that you are a keen football fan. You have a favourite team which you always support. In the past few months, your team has been doing rather well. It may be about to win a promotion. So you are feeling pretty happy about this. Well done lads! Keep going!

Question

A question for you to think about: To what extent was your team successful in improving its performance during the past season?

To answer this question, you need to do some serious, organised thinking. Start with what you know – the plain, honest facts. Things like the number of matches played, the wins, draws and defeats, the best players, the work of the manager and his training methods. Now, look at the question again. Looks pretty straightforward, doesn't it? You are being asked to explain how successful your team has been during the past football season. In other words, you are being asked to make a **judgement** about the team's performance, and to come to a **decision** about it.

So – how successful was the team? Was it, in fact, pretty hopeless? … not really very successful at all? Was the team actually brilliant? … the best it has ever played? Or was it partly successful? … very good in some areas, but with some weaknesses in others?

The central point is this: whatever answer you plan to give to this question, you are going to have to **justify** it. You are going to have to look, in some detail, at how your team has performed. For example:

◆ The manager – let's say he introduced some rigorous new training methods. You would certainly need to say what these were, and how well they worked.

◆ Now, how about the goalkeeper? Did he do well? Did he pull off some successful saves? Number of shut-outs?

◆ The defenders – did they work well together? Did they succeed in blocking attacks by opposing teams? Was the defence line effective, or does the team's record suggest that there are still some serious weaknesses?

◆ The forward line – let's say that the team has two new forwards. Do they work well together? Are they managing to cross the ball effectively? And how good is the scoring rate?

◆ Quality of opposition – were the team in a lower/higher division? Were the opponents affected by injuries or transfers to key players?

You are now well on your way to giving a clear and effective answer to the original question. You have probably noticed something interesting – you were making judgements about the different elements of the team. When you had to explain how good the defence was, you were **analysing** their performance. You looked at the performance of the defenders – let's say you found some effective performances, but you also noted some weaknesses which definitely needed some work. That is effective **assessment**! You believe that the forwards are working very well … you try to prove this by looking at shots at goal and actual goals scored … in other words, you are **arguing a case**, based on the evidence.

Let's keep this football analogy going a little longer. Suppose it was a slightly different question:

To what extent was the team's victory in the Cup Final due to the work of the forwards?

Again, you are being asked to make a judgement – to explain why the team won – but this time you are being given a definite indication, called an **isolated factor**, of the direction your explanation should be taking. You are certainly going to look at the work of the forwards, but you will also need to look at some of the other reasons for the team's success. So your answer might go a bit like this:

Answer

The forwards certainly made a major contribution to the team's victory, with effective passing, shots at goal and actual goals scored. Their role was therefore a very important one. However, the team's victory was also helped by other factors, and these must now be considered in turn. For example, the work of the midfield was vital: they kept the game moving, passing the ball on to the forwards. The defenders played a major role, blocking and spoiling strong attacking moves by the other team. The goalkeeper was excellent, pulling off at least one spectacular save. Finally, the careful build-up to the match – the training and coaching – brought the team to a new level of fitness and skill, and prepared them for victory.

You have deployed an extensive range of skills to help you focus on the issue in the question. You have analysed and evaluated the importance of each of the factors in the team's performance – you have made judgements. Most important of all, you have considered carefully the **isolated factor** given in the question, and worked to place it in the wider context of the full range of factors which led to the team's victory.

We can now leave the analogy of the football match. It is to be hoped that you have not found it trivial or childish, because it is certainly not intended to be so. Rather, we have used this to illustrate a very important and basic point in the approach to writing effective Higher History essays. There is no reason to be scared or nervous about how to write effective History essays, which are analytical and evaluative in style. Do not think of this style of writing as something which is awkward, cumbersome or, in some way, unnatural and difficult to use. The simple truth is that, in our everyday lives, we continually analyse and evaluate: it might be a football side's performance, a piece of music, a fashion style, the standard of catering at a restaurant – the list is endless.

Summary

In Higher History essays, you will be required to do the things which have been outlined in this chapter: analyse, evaluate, make judgements, place isolated factors in their wider contexts. These are skills which you already have developed, to some extent, and, as you work through the Higher History course, you will develop them further and become increasingly skilled at using them.

WRITING AN INTRODUCTION

How do I get started?

In the introduction to a History essay, you are doing something very significant – you are introducing your essay to the reader. This means that the introduction to the essay is really important, because it is going to give a first impression of what the essay is going to be like. It should give the reader an indication of how you are going to approach the subject, of some of the evidence that you might intend to use, and perhaps some idea of the possible arguments which you will make.

You may well be thinking that this is going to be difficult … you can't think how to write a good introduction … you can't think how to begin, how to get started … and if you can't think of a good introduction, then how on Earth are you going to manage to write a successful essay? Don't worry! Many students starting out on the Higher History course have faced this problem at the beginning of the course – nervousness about how to get started.

Like everything else, writing an effective introduction is something that can be learned – and practised. And, once you get the hang of it, you should find that it becomes fairly straightforward, almost something that you do as a matter of course.

Grabbing the reader's interest

To begin with, let's broaden the horizon a little. If you are attempting Higher History, that must mean that you are in 5th or 6th year – and that certainly means one thing. During this time, you have had a lot of experience of people, mainly your teachers, talking to you!

Let's think about this a little further. Think of sitting in a classroom, or better still a school assembly. A teacher, or head teacher, is planning to talk to you about something new, something that you have never heard of or come across before. In other words, they are **introducing** you to a new subject or topic. The subject or topic is probably quite important, and may well affect you directly. However, this is the first time that you have heard about it.

How did you react when the teacher or head teacher began to talk? You probably reacted in one of several ways:

◆ You were confused … you did not understand what the person was talking about … it did not seem to be making much sense to you. When the person finished talking, you were none the wiser. As an introduction, this did not work very well.

◆ You were bored … you could follow what the guy was saying, but, boy, was he ever dull! After a while, your attention began to wander … you lost interest in what he was saying. As an introduction, this did not work very well either.

WRITING AN INTRODUCTION

◆ You were interested … the speaker has caught your attention … he or she is setting out clearly and simply what they want to say … and they are holding your attention while they are doing it. You understand what they are saying … maybe you even want to find out more about it. As an introduction, this one worked!

Yes, we can all remember people talking to us like this, and the ones we remember best are the ones who held our interest, or who made us think! What they said was clear, it was straightforward, it was direct and it was focused.

 In other words, when you write the introduction to an essay, you should be trying to make as clear as possible what you are trying to say, and you should also be trying to hold the reader's interest. If you can manage to do this, you are probably on your way to writing a successful introduction, and, equally important, you have made a good start towards writing a successful essay!

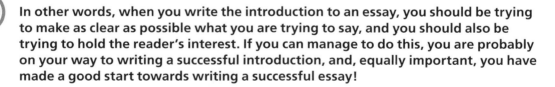

Key Points

In the introduction to your essay, there are **two** things you should be trying to do:

◆ You need to set out clearly how you propose to tackle the issue set in the title of the essay – i.e. make it clear to the reader of the essay (the person marking it) what you are planning to do.

◆ You also need to think about setting your essay in its wider context, so that you indicate clearly to the reader that you are aware of and have understood the issue, its implications and background.

Setting the issue in its wider context

In a Higher History essay it is very important to indicate that you are aware of the wider context of the issue about which you plan to write. The best place to do this is of course in the introduction.

It may help you to think of this as a kind of framework which will support and reinforce what you intend to say. You have an issue to tackle: this is the title of the essay. In your introduction, you need to show that you have understood the issue – for example, why the issue arose at this particular time, what was going on in the background. If you can do this, you are setting the issue in its wider context.

THE DEVELOPMENT SECTION

Now that we have spent some time on the introduction to your essay, it is time to move on to the development section. The development of your essay will be the largest and most substantial section of it. It is in this area that you will pick up most of the available marks, so you must try to get this as right as possible. If you do a good job in your development, you will be well on the way to completing a successful essay and to attaining a good mark.

So, what should an effective development look like? This is a question which is absolutely central.

You will have to focus directly on the issue being posed in the title. You will have to concentrate on **two** major areas in order to achieve success.

- ◆ **Knowledge** – you must make sure that you know and understand all the relevant **facts** which relate to the issue being posed in the question. If you demonstrate a sound grasp of the key areas of content required, of the basic knowledge and facts, then the person marking your essay can see that, at the very least, you know what you are talking about. This should give you a useful head start.

- ◆ **Analysis** and **evaluation** – you must now begin to use the all-important skills of analysis and evaluation, as you focus on the issue being posed in the question. Think back to the earlier sections, where we used the example of football to open up and explore this central factor in the writing of a successful History essay. As you have seen, these are skills which you have already learned and understood.

How much knowledge?

How much detail should you be trying to write in the development of your essay? This is a serious question, and one which always worries candidates sitting Higher History.

Think about it for a minute … You are a hard-working person. You are serious about Higher History. You have gone over all your notes, and worked very thoroughly on your revision guides. You want to do well in the exam. And now, here is Paper 1 of the Higher, and, for each essay, you have a maximum of 40 minutes. (In fact, by the time you have read through the paper, and decided which questions you wish to tackle, the time is more like 35 minutes!)

Not surprisingly, you might be a bit worried – are you going to manage to include all the relevant information within that time limit?

So, how much do you write? The only answer to this question is: as much as is necessary to answer the question. This may not seem to you to be much of an answer, but it is probably the best guidance that can be given.

You should try to realise that the questions in Paper 1 are fairly direct and specific. It should be fairly clear to you what you are being asked to write about. Also, the question-setters (the people who make up the exam paper) try hard to design questions which a young person aged 16 or 17 should be able to answer within the time limit.

Relevant knowledge

It is a further obvious point, of course, but one worth making. The knowledge which you deploy in your essay must be relevant to the question being asked. Material which is not relevant or which has been inserted to 'pad out' the essay, with a bit more detail, will simply not be recognised or rewarded, and will certainly do significant damage to your chances of success.

Demonstrating analysis and evaluation

So, how do you demonstrate that you can analyse and evaluate the issue being posed? Very simply, **by doing what the question is asking you to do**! Work out what the question is asking you to do – you may be asked to make a judgement about something, or to consider the significance of a specific isolated factor alongside a number of others.

The central point is that you work out very clearly and definitely what you are being asked to do. Once you have decided this, and got it clear in your mind, you can make rapid progress.

You now understand what the question is asking you to do – so do it! Focus directly on **answering the question** – do what it is asking you to – and you will quickly realise that you are using **analysis** and **evaluation**. You are addressing the issue posed in the question, in the terms in which it has been set – and the only way you can do this is to analyse and evaluate.

A successful development section

So, to pull all this together, what makes a successful development? First of all, the development must have a very clear and definite focus on the question, showing that the candidate has understood what the question is asking them to do.

The most effective developments are those which show clear and accurate **knowledge** of the issue. The candidate will have demonstrated a thorough knowledge of the key facts and issues relating to the question. The evidence being presented will be both accurate and relevant. Above all, there will be no irrelevant material.

It will also be clear that the candidate has worked hard to do exactly what the question has asked them to. By doing this, there is ample demonstration and illustration of the skills of **analysis** and **evaluation**. Knowledge is used to clearly illustrate, support and reinforce the analysis and evaluation points being made. Candidates who **use their knowledge to address the issue** being posed in the question are far more likely to write successful essays.

THE CONCLUSION

The conclusion to your essay will be the overall answer to the question. It is what your essay should have been working towards, right from the start.

Think about what you have done already:

The introduction

You have identified clearly what the essay title is asking you to do; you have given some indication of how you intend to tackle the essay; and you have established the background to the subject – that is, you have set the essay in its wider context.

The development

In the development, you have tackled the key areas of content and analysis which are central to the structure of your essay. You will have been analysing, evaluating, making judgements, as required, on the range of factors and issues related to the essay subject. You will have deployed or used evidence or factual knowledge as you think necessary and appropriate.

Above all, you will have done what the essay title has asked you to do. If you were asked to consider the development of a trend, you have done that. If you were asked to consider the significance of an isolated factor in causing something, you have done that.

However, you have now done most of the heavy work in bringing this essay towards its completion. It is now time to start drawing things together – it is time to write the **conclusion**.

A balanced conclusion

There has to be a conclusion, an overall answer to the question. The person marking your essay needs to see clearly that you have understood the question, and that you have made a real effort to answer the question. If there is no conclusion, you will miss out on some of the marks awarded for the structure of your essay.

So could the conclusion just be a single sentence? Yes, that could be one way to write the conclusion – but probably it would not be particularly effective, and you would lose out on the marks available.

You should definitely be trying to write a **balanced conclusion**, where, once again, you have a clear focus and concentration on what the essay has asked you to do. You are demonstrating to the marker that you have thought carefully and clearly about the essay you are writing, and that you are now attempting to pull your thoughts together.

A balanced conclusion should follow naturally from the development of the essay. You should be aiming towards this all the way through. In the development section, you have kept a clear focus on the question: you have been deploying your knowledge to address the issues, as you analyse, evaluate and make judgements. You have been very clear all along where you are trying to go with this essay.

So if the essay was asking you to make a judgement about something, that is what you have done. If you were asked to evaluate a trend or a development over a period of time, you have made a genuine attempt to do that. If the title asked you to consider an isolated factor, you have done so, widening the context to include other related factors.

In other words, **you have done what the essay question asked you to do.**

In the conclusion, you are now going to bring all your thoughts together, and come to an overall answer to the question, based on what you have already written in the development.

You are going to revisit, briefly, the points that you made there, in order to remind the marker that you have kept a clear focus on the issue while you were working through the essay. If you were asked to make a judgement about something, you are now going to make that judgement. If it was a case of evaluating a trend or development, you now can make that evaluation. If you were given an isolated factor to consider, you are going to do that, and, of course, make a comment on other, related factors.

This, then, is your **balanced conclusion**. You have examined the evidence that you have presented, and you have considered, analysed and evaluated each piece of it in turn. You have made it very obvious to the marker, all along, that you have a very clear focus on the issue contained in the title. You are now going to demonstrate where this process has taken you – you come to an **overall judgement** on the issue – your balanced conclusion. You can now bring your essay to a successful finish.

Hints and Tips

Without a doubt, getting clear from the start what you are being asked to do is the single most important thing you have to do as you consider writing a History essay. If you can get this right, you have made the first step towards writing a successful Higher History essay.

Decide what you are being asked to do.

Read the title of the essay very carefully.

Now, read it again – and focus very clearly on the **exact wording** of the title:

What **subject** is it asking about?

What is it asking you to do?

WORKED EXAMPLE OF A HIGHER HISTORY ESSAY

At this stage, the best approach is to have a look at an actual Higher History essay, from a recent examination paper. This example comes from the section dealing with Later Modern History – it's on a popular topic!

Example

To what extent were the Liberal social reforms of 1906–14 a response to the challenge from the Labour Party?

So, what are you being asked to do?

You are being asked to think about the **reasons** why the Liberal Government of 1906–14 introduced social reforms and, in particular, **how much** of this was the result of the growing challenge from the Labour Party.

This is one of the standard styles of Higher History questions: this is an **issue** with a very clear **isolated factor**.

The **subject** is now quite clear: the **reasons** for the Liberal reforms.

The **isolated factor** has been clearly established: the challenge from the Labour Party.

So, what are you being asked to do?

◆ You are being asked to look at the **reasons** why the Liberal Government of 1906–14 introduced their social reforms.

◆ Decide how much of this was due to the challenge from the Labour Party.

◆ Look at other reasons why the social reforms were introduced.

◆ Reach some kind of decision about **how important** the challenge from Labour was. Was it the main reason for the reforms? Was the Labour challenge one of a number of reasons? Or was it a fairly minor reason?

Introduction

Let's think about introducing this subject to the reader – remembering, of course, that the person who is going to read this essay is also the **marker**. Let's remind ourselves about what we should be trying to do in an introduction. There are several important things which should be done:

◆ Show that we have understood the question – that we understand what the question is asking us to do.

◆ Set the issue in its wider context.

◆ Give some kind of indication of how we are going to approach the issue – of the likely approach to be taken by the essay.

So, in this essay, we might begin by stating, briefly, that between 1906 and 1914, the Liberal Government did, in fact, introduce an important series of social reforms.

> At this time, the Labour Party was beginning to challenge the Liberal Party for the votes of working-class people, and this challenge was clearly an important factor in motivating the Liberal Government to introduce its reforms.
>
> However, there were several other important factors at work, such as concern about the levels of poverty, issues of national security and efficiency, and the changes in political ideas related to the growth of New Liberalism.
>
> All of these clearly influenced the decision by the Liberal Government to introduce social reforms.

Is this a successful introduction? Does it show **understanding of the issue**? We have shown that the essay will have a clear focus on the **reasons** why the Liberals introduced their social reforms, in particular the challenge from the Labour Party.

What about the **wider context**? We have indicated that there were other factors which influenced the Liberals to introduce social reforms.

Does it show an indication of **the likely approach to be taken**? It should be clear to the reader that this essay intends to assess the impact of the Labour challenge, in the broader perspective of the other factors.

An introduction that does these things is likely to be quite effective.

Development

The challenge from Labour

Yes, the growth of the Labour Party was regarded as a real threat by the Liberals. The Labour Party was making a strong push to attract working-class voters in areas such as south Wales, the north of England, and central Scotland. These were areas of Britain which traditionally supported the Liberal Party, and the Liberals could clearly not afford to lose support from these voters.

So, for the Liberal Party, it clearly made a great deal of electoral sense to come up with ideas and policies which were attractive to working-class voters – to give these voters an incentive to support the Liberal Party – an incentive such as the range of social reforms introduced between 1906 and 1914, which were clearly designed to support and help poorer, working-class people.

It is clear, then, that the challenge from the Labour Party was a major factor in the decision by the Liberals to introduce social reforms. The reforms were popular with the working class, and would be likely to help the Liberals win votes among them.

Clearly, however, there were other factors which motivated the Liberals to bring in their social reforms, and we shall now look at some of them.

The investigations into poverty

The investigations by Booth and Rowntree into the causes and nature of poverty took place at this time, and certainly had a major impact on the Liberal Party. The detailed reports on the lives of the poor in London and York caused a sensation. Up to this point, no one had suspected that poverty existed on such a level and affected such large numbers.

The Booth and Rowntree investigations presented a frightening illustration of the real levels of poverty in British society at the time. Before these investigations, there had been some general assumptions made about poverty: that it was largely restricted to the poorer parts of great cities like London, and that most people fell into poverty due to their own stupidity and wastefulness.

The Booth and Rowntree investigations changed all that. It was now clear that poverty had real causes – low wages, sickness, unemployment, old age – and that people who fell into poverty had little or no control over these causes.

The Booth and Rowntree investigations were far too important to be ignored. When the Liberal Party formed the government in 1906, their decision to introduce social reforms was certainly massively influenced by the work of Booth and Rowntree.

The Boer War: the issue of national security

The war against the Boers in South Africa raised a number of problems for Britain, and one of the most serious of these was the fact that substantial numbers of recruits for the army had to be rejected on medical grounds – they were simply not fit enough. The worrying fact for Britain was that these men came from the poorest areas of the country – from backgrounds of low wages and poor-quality housing.

For Britain, this was serious. Suppose, at some time in the future, Britain had to fight a large-scale war, against powerful enemies. The country could face disastrous defeat because it did not have sufficient numbers of able-bodied soldiers.

Clearly, something would have to be done – and fairly quickly. The most obvious thing was to do something about improving the lives of the poorest people in Britain.

National efficiency

At the end of the nineteenth century, the British manufacturing industry was facing serious competition from other countries, in particular from Germany. German factories were producing better-quality products, and producing them more quickly and more cheaply. Britain was losing customers. Germany was doing much better than Britain. Investigations showed that German factories were more efficient and so were German workers.

Significantly, Germany had introduced social reforms in the 1880s to give its workers a certain amount of social security, such as sickness benefit and retirement rights. In Britain there had been many arguments against this: for example, workers would become lazy, they would stop saving money. The example of Germany now seemed to disprove this. German industry was highly effective, with excellent production from its factories. It could be argued that the German system of social security was actually helping this, by reducing some of the worst aspects of poverty, and by demonstrating that the state would support its citizens when they faced problems, such as sickness and old age.

It was, of course, argued that Britain would benefit if a similar system of social security was introduced to support British workers. Clearly, the issue of national efficiency was a further factor motivating the Liberals to introduce social reforms.

'New' Liberalism

During the nineteenth century, it was widely accepted that people took charge of their own lives and supported themselves, and that it was not the job of the state to interfere in this. However, at the start of the twentieth century, a change of view began to develop, particularly among some leading members of the Liberal Party. Men such as Herbert Asquith, David Lloyd George and Winston Churchill began to argue that it should, in fact, become the job of the state to provide financial support for its citizens – certainly at the times when they faced difficulties and hardship, such as in sickness, unemployment and old age. These 'New' Liberals believed that it should be the **duty** of the state to do this.

These men, and others, were highly successful and influential Members of Parliament. They became leading members of the Liberal Government when it took office in 1906. Not surprisingly, their ideas and beliefs had a major impact on what the Liberal Government actually did – on the series of social reforms introduced between 1906 and 1908.

> ### Key Points
>
> The Liberal social reforms: factors identified
> - the Labour challenge
> - the Booth and Rowntree reports
> - the impact of the Boer War
> - national efficiency
> - 'New' Liberalism.

Now, complete this exercise by writing down the headings in the Key Points box above. Beside each of the factors identified, write down briefly how you think it influenced the decision by the Liberal Government to introduce social reforms.

As you are doing this, something very important is happening. You are now analysing, evaluating and arguing the evidence which you have assembled and deployed! You are doing all the things you need to do to score a good result in a Higher History essay.

Go back to the original title. You were given an **isolated factor** to think about: the importance of the challenge of the Labour Party in the decision by the Liberal Government to introduce social reforms. Perhaps you are now ready to answer this question!

So – the challenge of the Labour Party? Well, obviously it was an important reason driving the Liberals to introduce social reform. Like all politicians, the Liberals needed to persuade voters to support them. They were certainly getting worried that a rival party, Labour, was starting to pick up support. The Liberal Government's social reforms can be seen as intended to help poorer people with their problems. However, they can also be regarded as a very shrewd move by the Party – giving an incentive to working-class voters to continue voting Liberal, and not turn to the Labour Party.

We can now see and understand that, while the challenge from the Labour Party was certainly a very important reason motivating the Liberals to introduce social reforms, it was certainly not the **only** reason. We have identified at least **four** further reasons for the introduction of the reforms: the Booth and Rowntree reports, the impact of the Boer War, concerns about national efficiency and the development of 'New' Liberalism.

This is now beginning to shape up as a fairly successful development section. We have identified a number of factors relevant to the issue, and we have examined each of them in turn, closely relating what we have written to the actual question. It is now time to think of pulling things together, and making a final return to the issue. In other words, it is time to think of the **conclusion**.

Conclusion

The most successful conclusions are the ones that come naturally from the development of the essay. We have considered carefully the **isolated factor** which we were given at the start, and then gone on to consider a number of other factors, all within the context of the issue.

So – what conclusion have we reached?

> Clearly, the challenge to the Liberal Party from Labour was a major factor in causing the Liberals to introduce social reforms – the challenge was a serious one. However, there were at least four other factors in play at the same time: the investigations into poverty, national security, national efficiency and New Liberalism. It is clear, from what has been set out in the development of this essay, that **all** of them were significant. They were all key factors in the Liberal Government's decision to proceed with social reforms. The challenge from Labour was one of a number of key factors leading to the social reforms.

This is a good, effective conclusion to the essay. It has followed naturally from the development – it makes sense to the person reading it. It is a clear, overall answer to the question in the title, and brings the essay to a satisfactory ending.

WHAT MAKES A GOOD ESSAY?

Let's get some practice

Throughout this section we have emphasised the key point in the writing of a successful Higher History essay – the importance of **doing what the question asks you to do**. You can now get some practice in this basic skill of essay writing.

On the next few pages, there are examples of Higher History essay titles, taken from recent SQA papers. The titles are selected from Medieval History, Early Modern History and Later Modern History, and from a wide range of contexts.

Here is what you should try to do. For each title:

◆ Work out what you are being asked to do.

◆ Make up an outline answer: outline, briefly, the **content** or **evidence** that you would use and then, briefly, how you would use it to **answer the question** in the title.

For Practice

Medieval History

1. How important was the need to develop the Scottish economy as a motive for strengthening the powers of the Crown during the reigns of David I and Henry II?

2. How successfully did Henry II and David I overcome the challenges that faced the monarchy?

3. To what extent was the secular church more important than the regular church in the Middle Ages?

4. How important was the Peasants' Revolt in causing the decline of feudal society?

5. 'Brutal, poor and without hope.' How accurate is this view of the lives of peasants during the Middle Ages?

Early Modern History

1. How important were financial issues as a source of disagreement between James VI and his English Parliament?

2. To what extent was religion the main cause of the outbreak of civil war in England?

3. How successful was the Glorious Revolution in limiting the powers of the Crown?

4. To what extent was the failure of constitutional monarchy in France in 1792 a result of the pressure of war?

For Practice continued ➤

For Practice continued

5. To what extent had French society been changed by the Revolution in the period up to 1799?

Later Modern History

1. How democratic had Britain become by 1928?

2. To what extent was the growth of democracy in Britain after 1860 due to social and economic change?

3. How important were economic factors in the growth of national feeling in Germany during the period 1815–1850?

4. How important was the leadership of Hitler in the rise of the Nazis to power in Germany by 1933?

5. To what extent did the Nazis' control of Germany up to 1933 depend on their social and economic policies?

6. How important was the role of Piedmont in the achievement of Italian unification by 1871?

7. How successful were the Civil Rights movements of the 1950s and 1960s in achieving their aims?

8. 'The power of the Tsarist state was relatively unchanged after the 1905 Revolution.' How accurate is this view?

Outline answers

Medieval History

> 1. How important was the need to develop the Scottish economy as a motive for strengthening the powers of the Crown during the reigns of David I and Henry II?

During the reigns of David I and Henry II, the powers of the Crown in both Scotland and England were strengthened significantly. In this essay, you are being asked to explain how much of this was due to the need to develop the economy, the isolated factor provided in the title. You need to evaluate the need for economic development in the context of the question, and then consider other factors, such as the administration of justice.

2. **How successfully did Henry II and David I overcome the challenges that faced the monarchy?**

Both David I and Henry II faced a number of challenges when they became king, in areas such as the administration of royal justice and the power of the church. In this essay, you need to think of defining these challenges, and how the kings attempted to deal with them. Overall, you should be attempting to assess and analyse their level of success in dealing with the challenges.

3. **To what extent was the secular church more important than the regular church in the Middle Ages?**

During the Middle Ages, the regular church and the secular church both fulfilled significant roles. You are being asked to make a judgement, or assessment, as to whether the secular church was more important. Clearly, this can be approached in a number of ways, by considering such issues as the work of the church in education and learning, care of the sick, supporting the poor, social control, economic development, and so on.

4. **How important was the Peasants' Revolt in causing the decline of feudal society?**

In the later Middle Ages, the institution of serfdom began a significant decline. In this essay you are being asked to make a judgement as to how much of this decline was due to the growth of social unrest, as evidenced by the Peasants' Revolt. You will also have to think about other factors and their role in the decline of feudal society, such as economic changes and the impact of the Black Death.

5. **'Brutal, poor and without hope.' How accurate is this view of the lives of peasants during the Middle Ages?**

Once more, you will have to make a judgement or assessment. You will have to make clear how accurate it is to sum up the lives of peasants in the terms of the question, as being 'brutal, poor and without hope'. You need to be able to explain and justify the statement, and any qualification you may wish to make about it. For example, can you deploy evidence and argument that peasant life was better than this? Again, you need to think of providing both evidence and analysis.

Early Modern History

1. **How important were financial issues as a source of disagreement between James VI and his English Parliament?**

    James VI and I had a series of disagreements and disputes with his English Parliament. You are being asked to think about how much these difficulties and problems were due to issues of finance. You can then move on to look at other reasons for disagreement between James and Parliament, for example on matters of religion. Overall, you will need to think about the importance of finance in the wider context of disputes between James and his Parliament.

2. **To what extent was religion the main cause of the outbreak of civil war in England?**

    In this essay, you are given an isolated factor to think about: the significance of religion as a cause of the English Civil War. Of course, religious issues were important at the time, and you will need to address their degree of importance. In addition, you need to consider other causes of the conflict – for example, the question of royal power – and relate these to the overall issue posed in the question.

3. **How successful was the Glorious Revolution in limiting the powers of the Crown?**

    Here you are asked to make a judgement or assessment about the extent to which the powers of the Crown were limited, following the Glorious Revolution. A successful approach might be to consider different aspects of Crown powers in turn, and the extent to which they were limited: financial powers, military power, control of foreign policy, and so on.

4. **To what extent was the failure of constitutional monarchy in France in 1792 a result of the pressure of war?**

    The attempts to establish a constitutional monarchy in France ended in failure in 1792. In this essay, you are being asked to explain the reasons for this failure, paying special attention to the isolated factor given in the title – the pressure of war. Having done this, you then need to think about other factors which contributed to the failure of the constitutional monarchy. For example, you might consider here the role of the émigrés; royalist intrigues; the Flight to Varennes; the growing unpopularity of the King and Queen, particularly Marie Antoinette; and wider political changes taking place in France.

5. **To what extent had French society been changed by the Revolution in the period up to 1799?**

In this essay, you are being asked to make a judgement about the extent to which society had been changed due to the effects of the Revolution. A useful approach might be to look at political, economic and social changes which had taken place. For example, you might consider how political rights were developed and changed; the extent to which wealth was re-distributed; land ownership; the role of the church; how the lives of different social classes were affected – the bourgeoisie, the sans-culottes. In addition to this, you might well deal with aspects of French society which were perhaps relatively unchanged by the Revolution.

Later Modern History

1. **How democratic had Britain become by 1928?**

Here you are being asked to make a judgement: how democratic was Britain by 1928? Was it completely democratic, or were there still some limitations? Your best approach here might be to think about different aspects of democracy in turn: the right to vote, fairness at elections, the right to become an MP, and so on.

2. **To what extent was the growth of democracy in Britain after 1860 due to social and economic change?**

In this essay, you are clearly being asked to consider the reasons for the growth of democracy, and you are given the isolated factor of social and economic change to deal with first: for example, the impact of industry, the growth of towns and cities, the railways. You can then think of other factors which promoted and encouraged democracy: political movements such as trade unions and women's movements, the spread of education and literacy, political self-interest and the impact of the First World War.

3. **How important were economic factors in the growth of national feeling in Germany during the period 1815–1850?**

Again, you are given an isolated factor to consider first: the impact of economic factors in the growth of national feeling in Germany. So you might begin by considering the impact of the *Zollverein*, and possibly railways. Then you could move on to other factors influencing nationalism: political pressures, the impact of the French invasions, cultural nationalism.

4. How important was the leadership of Hitler in the rise of the Nazis to power in Germany by 1933?

This essay is concentrating on the reasons for the rise of the Nazis to power by 1933. Clearly there were a number of important reasons for this, including the isolated factor which you are given: Hitler's leadership. Having considered this, you can then move on to other factors, and consider them in turn: resentment at the Treaty of Versailles, the economic problems of 1923 and the early 1930s, divisions among opponents, and other related factors.

5. To what extent did the Nazis' control of Germany up to 1933 depend on their social and economic policies?

In this essay, you are again given a clear isolated factor to think about: the extent to which Nazi social and economic policies enabled them to maintain control of Germany. So you might well begin by looking at issues such as job creation and the reduction of unemployment, and attitudes towards women. Following this, you would probably move on to think about other things which assisted their hold on power – propaganda, anti-Semitism, control of youth, political repression, the use of terror.

6. How important was the role of Piedmont in the achievement of Italian unification by 1871?

Italian unification and the role played by Piedmont: you are being asked to think about the reasons for the development of unification. Clearly, Piedmont, under the leadership of Cavour, played a highly significant role: this is given as an isolated factor for you to consider. So also did other factors – mistakes made by Austria, the campaigns of Garibaldi, the intervention of other powers – and you would move on to each of these, and other factors, in turn.

7. How successful were the Civil Rights movements of the 1950s and 1960s in achieving their aims?

In this essay, you are being asked to make a judgement about the level of success of the Civil Rights movements in achieving their aims. Clearly, it would be important here to establish what their aims were: voting rights, ending segregation, equal opportunities in employment and education. It would also be a good idea to identify some of the important strands within Civil Rights: the NAACP, the SCLC, SNCC, the 'Freedom Rides', the black radical movements. Having done this, you would then need to make your judgement about the extent of their success – the various pieces of legislation dealing with Civil Rights, the desegregation of schools, voting rights. It might also be worthwhile to look at the range of problems which the Civil Rights movements were trying to tackle – political and social segregation in the Southern states; economic disadvantage in the North.

8. 'The power of the Tsarist state was relatively unchanged after the 1905 Revolution.' How accurate is this view?

In this essay you have to come to a judgement, or argue a case, about the extent to which the power of the Tsarist state was unchanged following the Revolution of 1905. You need to think about whether the Revolution led to significant changes in Tsarist power: for example, through the creation of the Duma. Then you might move on to think about issues such as the work of Stolypin, the church, the opposition groups. Can you find evidence of a significant reduction in Tsarist power, or was it largely unchanged?

SECTION 2

Source Questions

SOURCE HANDLING SKILLS

In Paper 2 of the Higher History examination, you will have to write answers to four questions. These four questions will relate to five sources on the specific topic you are studying. This paper is worth 30 marks in total, so makes up 30 per cent of your total mark. Two questions will be worth 5 marks and two questions will be worth 10 marks. It is essential that your four answers are as good as you can possibly make them.

Primary sources and secondary sources

What are the kinds of sources that historians use to study history? At the most basic level, sources are divided into the categories of *primary* and *secondary*. You will probably be familiar with these terms:

◆ A primary source was produced at the time an event in the past was happening or by someone who experienced the event at a later date.

◆ Secondary sources are written by people, normally historians, after the event, but they are about the past.

The sources that you will study will normally be **written**, but on occasion you may be asked to analyse a photograph or other **visual** source.

Remember that primary sources are not always superior in understanding and accuracy to secondary sources. Very often historians have the benefit of hindsight and access to a wider range of evidence than the people writing at the time of the event. This might mean that

historians know the consequences of what is being described and that they are aware of a range of information that the people writing at the time of the event simply could not know. This can give historians considerable advantages when commenting on the past.

A skill worth having?

Absolutely! Learning how to interpret presented information in a critical way is a very useful skill. It is important for many subjects, not just History! Just think about what a police officer or lawyer has to do with evidence, for example. It will be helpful for study at university and for life. History teaches us to be critical, and at a time when we have access to a lot of information from television, the Internet, etc, the ability to interpret and criticise is vital.

However, what historians write deserves to be critically assessed like any other source. They can get things wrong and they certainly disagree with each other! The important thing to remember is to **evaluate sources** in the light of your understanding of the period you have studied. Your assessment of the source is valid as long as you can properly justify it based on the available evidence, and your broader recalled knowledge.

What You Should Know

With the exception of the comparison question, all of the source questions require you to accurately apply recalled knowledge. You should remember to use recalled evidence when supporting your answer. Recalled knowledge can be used to extend and explain points from the source as well as to supply new information that is not included in the source, but is relevant to the question.

Paper 2: The 'Scottish' paper

Paper 2 is a source-based examination that assesses key periods from Scotland's past. Students have a choice of five topics for study. You will be studying one of the following topics:

◆ Special Topic 1: The Wars of Independence, 1286–1328

◆ Special Topic 2: The Age of Reformation, 1542–1603

◆ Special Topic 3: The Treaty of Union, 1689–1740

◆ Special Topic 4: Migration and Empire, 1830–1939

◆ Special Topic 5: Scotland and the Impact of the Great War, 1914–1928

How will the exam paper be structured?

For each of the topics studied there is a detailed summary of the content to be covered. The following table gives the content for the Impact of the Great War, 1914–1928.

Issue	Detailed content
Background	Scotland on the eve of the Great War: political, social and economic conditions; martial traditions

Issue	Detailed content
1. Scots on the Western Front	Voluntary recruitment; the experience of Scots on the Western Front, with reference to the battles of Loos and the Somme; the kilted regiments; the role of Scottish military personnel in terms of commitment, casualties, leadership and overall contribution to the military effort
2. Domestic impact of war: society and culture	Recruitment and conscription; pacifism and conscientious objection; DORA; changing role of women in wartime, including rent strikes; scale and effects of military losses on Scottish society; commemoration and remembrance
3. Domestic impact of war: industry and economy	Effects of war on industry, agriculture and fishing; price rises and rationing; post-war economic change and difficulties; post-war emigration; the land issue in the Highlands and Islands
4. Domestic impact of war: politics	The impact of the war on political developments as exemplified by the growth of radicalism, the ILP and Red Clydeside, continuing support for political unionism and the crisis of Scottish identity
Perspective	The significance of the Great War in the development of Scottish identity

The other four topics also have content described like this.

The background and perspective sections of the topics will not be examined. They are there to give you context for the topic and allow you to reflect on the importance of the event in Scottish history.

Within each topic area there are four **general issues**, as seen in the left-hand column. Each of these is developed into specific sub-issues to be studied through the content, listed in the right-hand column. We will look next at how each of these overall issues and specific sub-issues are used when examiners make up questions.

Issues and sub-issues

The descriptor on pages 40–41 gives overall issues and detailed content for one topic.

These issues and content are used when making up questions. This will help you to limit the content you have to learn. Your teacher/lecturer will have given you these for the topic you are studying.

For the Impact of the Great War, the following issues and sub-issues have been created. Only the first issue is given as an example.

Overall Issue 1: Scots on the Western Front.

◆ How fully does Source A show the involvement of Scots on the Western Front?

The detailed content gives three sub-issues that start with the stem 'How far…':

◆ How far does Source B give the reasons why so many Scots volunteered to fight in the Great War?

◆ How far does Source C illustrate the experiences of Scots on the Western Front?

◆ How far does Source D give evidence of the contribution of Scots to the military effort on the Western Front?

Each issue in each topic area is developed in this way. The reason for this will become clear when we look at the questions. A detailed list of the issues and sub-issues for each topic can be found in the Appendix.

Remember

The next section of the book will tell you about the different questions. However, it is important to remember that all four of the main issues will be assessed in the final examination.

Question types

There will be *four* questions testing your source handling skills. The good news is that the wording of the questions is standard – you can get used to the kinds of questions in advance and be ready to answer them. They will be used in the other four topic areas as well. We have already seen examples of the 'How fully' and 'How far' questions. Here are all four of the question types:

1. How useful is Source V…?

2. To what extent do Source W and Source X agree…?

3. How fully does Source Y…?

4. How far does Source Z…?

The point of these questions is to test your ability to do three things:

◆ Evaluate a source.

◆ Compare sources.

◆ Put a source in its context.

In order to successfully answer these questions, you need to use the right approach and show the right level of knowledge.

Answer The Question (ATQ)

In the first section of work on essays you were told how important it is to Answer The Question. Exactly the same is true when answering source questions. If you do NOT answer the question you will get some credit for selecting the correct information (assuming you have done this) but you will not get the high marks you want.

You need to think about what the question is asking you to do. Is it asking you to **evaluate** the source, or to **compare** two sources, or to discuss a source in its **context**? That is what the marker is going to be looking for. If you just give facts from the source and from your knowledge, you have not answered the question directly. Even if the evidence you write about is relevant to the question, if you have not done what the question is asking you to do, you will not achieve full marks.

SOURCE EVALUATION QUESTIONS

Why do I need to evaluate a source?

This is a basic question for historians looking at source material. Historians need to develop the ability to be critical with the evidence they are faced with. It is important not to accept evidence just because you are told it is useful.

Think about all the aspects of a source that might be important:

◆ the time when a source is produced

◆ who is telling us the information

◆ the content – it can give us clues about the view of the author

◆ what is not there – because any source only gives part of the picture.

So historians must assess **how useful** a source is for the study of a particular topic. The **source evaluation question** will always begin: 'How useful is Source A/B/C as evidence of…?'

In the Higher History exam, questions that evaluate the usefulness of sources will relate to one of the general issues or specific sub-issues.

For the 'How useful' question you will need to explain whether or not the source is **useful** in explaining an event or development. Don't forget to ATQ!

Remember, a source for this sort of question can only give us **part** of the picture (historians write complete books to explain developments and events), so a source is only going to be able to tell us part of the answer.

Good practice

A sentence that says, 'Source A is useful for explaining … but it does not tell us the whole story …' is providing an **evaluation**. The marker knows from this sentence that you understand there is a bigger picture than the source is telling.

Bad practice

If, on the other hand, you say, 'Source A describes developments … but it does not tell us about …', you are **simply describing** the source and the gaps in it. This does not answer the question directly.

Hints and Tips

Underneath each question in the exam paper there is a prompt to help you. It tells you what the examiners are looking for. Here is the prompt for the 'How useful…?' question:

In reaching a conclusion you should refer to:
- *the origin and possible purpose of the source*
- *the content of the source*
- *recalled knowledge.*

How are answers to the source evaluation question marked?

The person who marks your exam paper has to put in a bit of work too! In order to decide what marks your answer will get, markers can use a grid like the one below. It helps them to spot and assess what they are looking for.

There are five marks allocated to this question.

Feature of marking	Mark allocation	Marks given	Overall mark
Evaluation of provenance	Up to 2 marks		
Evaluation of content	Up to 2 marks		
Evaluation of relevant recalled knowledge	Up to 2 marks		

As you can see, up to two marks can be given for each of the features that the marker is looking for. This allows you to reach the five allocated marks in a number of ways.

Evaluation of provenance

Provenance means **origin** and **purpose**, and up to two marks may be given for points you make about these. In order to get two marks, you need to give some explanation about the usefulness of the origin and purpose. This will depend on the particular source you are evaluating. You need to tailor your comments to fit the particular source and question.

Evaluation of content

You can get up to two marks for indicating which parts of the source you consider are useful in terms of the question. In order to get full marks, you would need to mention each point separately **and** explain its usefulness. Just listing the points will only get you one mark.

Sources will contain **three** distinct points of content that you can earn credit for mentioning and explaining. They will also contain material that is not relevant to the question. Do not be distracted by this! Be careful when selecting the information you are going to mention. Make sure it is relevant to the question.

Evaluation of relevant recalled knowledge

You can also get two marks by showing your recall of relevant knowledge. You can do this by developing the points in the source further, or by introducing new knowledge that the source does not contain. Remember – in order to gain the marks, you have to develop the points **in terms of the question**.

Hints and Tips

For the evaluation question, it is good practice to finish with an overall sentence summing up the answer.

Remember

Here is a useful checklist for answering the evaluation question:

◆ Come to a **judgement** on the usefulness of the source in terms of the overall question.

◆ Comment on the **origin** and **purpose** of the source in terms of its usefulness.

◆ Identify the **main relevant points** made in the presented source and comment on these.

◆ Identify areas that **extend** the points in the source, or that are not mentioned in the source but relate to the question.

◆ Conclude, giving an **overall judgement**.

Understanding what the marker expects

The person who marks your exam paper has to follow guidelines on what to look for in each answer. It's not up to the individual marker. For each question, marking instructions are given. It is useful to understand precisely what this means, as it can help you to tailor your answer in the correct way. So, let's get inside the mind of a Higher History marker!

Here is an example of a source, question and marking scheme from Special Topic 4: Migration and Empire, 1830–1939.

Example

Source A: from an advertisement placed in the *John O'Groat Journal*, 22 January 1841, by Duncan McLennan, Emigrant Agent, Inverness.

Emigration to the British Settlements of North America

Arrangements have been made for a succession of ships in the course of the ensuing Spring, for the conveyance of Passengers from Cromarty, Thurso and any other place where a sufficient number of Passengers may offer, to ports in Nova Scotia and Lower Canada. Here it need only be remarked, the climate is excellent, the soil fertile, and the commodities of life abundant, they abound with numerous safe bays, and the coast in general affords fishing ground scarcely surpassed by any in the world. A Central Emigration Committee has been formed in Toronto, Upper Canada in order that, by constant communication and mutual arrangements, every facility may be offered to emigrants on their arrival, as to their location, settlement, and employment.

How useful is **Source A** as evidence of the opportunities that attracted Scots to other lands? (5 marks)

In reaching a conclusion you should refer to:
◆ *the origin and possible purpose of the source*
◆ *the content of the source*
◆ *recalled knowledge.*

At this point it is useful to have some inside knowledge of the marker's instructions, which say:

'The candidate makes a judgement on how useful Source A is as evidence of the opportunities that attracted Scots to other lands, in terms of…'

The marker is going to look in your answer for certain points from Source A which show that you have picked out and interpreted the significant issues:

◆ **Origin**: advertisement by an emigrant agent.
◆ **Possible purpose**: to attract Scottish emigrants by emphasising the ease of getting to Canada and the possibilities of life there.
◆ **Content**:
  ➢ Ships have been organised to convey people from Cromarty, Thurso and other places to Canada.
  ➢ Attractions of Nova Scotia and Lower Canada: climate, fertile soil and good fishing.
  ➢ Emigration committee formed to help emigrants on their arrival with location, settlement and employment.

So far, so good. The next thing the marker is going to look for is points from your recalled knowledge which support and develop the points in the source. This could include:

◆ Domineering landlords and lack of real opportunities encouraged emigration from Highlands of Scotland.
◆ The New Zealand Company promoted emigration and offered assisted passages.
◆ *Chambers's Edinburgh Journal* promoted emigration to Canada.

These are all points that show your knowledge of the topic. Now for some points that show your knowledge of the wider context. This could include:

◆ The British American Land Company attracted large numbers of emigrant Scots to Canada and sponsored emigration.

◆ The promise of land ownership attracted impoverished Scots to Canada.

◆ The benefits of Canadian land ownership were constantly promoted in Scottish press.

◆ The promise of independence and modest prosperity were promoted by the report of the Napier Commission.

◆ The Homestead Act of 1862 encouraged Scottish emigration to America.

◆ The Australian Company of Edinburgh and Leith promoted Canada's fertile soil and healthy climate, along with its large mineral deposits and good transport facilities.

◆ Large numbers of impoverished Highlanders travelled to Australia through assisted passage schemes.

◆ The Highland and Island Emigration Society contrasted Scottish poverty and Australian prosperity to promote emigration.

◆ New Zealand was promoted as having a very healthy climate and fertile soil on cheap land.

◆ Scottish craftsmen were enticed to the USA by high wages during the nineteenth century.

◆ Scottish colliers were lured across the Atlantic by high wages, quick passages on ships and personal recommendations.

◆ Material gain was the driving force for most emigrants.

◆ Scots were lured overseas by a variety of economic, social and cultural inducements.

◆ For a minority, foreign fields offered an opportunity for financial investment.

◆ Among the incentives to leave Scotland were the anticipation of the neighbourliness, co-operation and familiarity of an established Scottish settlement.

◆ Any other relevant factors.

Key Points

◆ This is from the first issue, on migration of the Scots, from the Migration and Empire topic. The question is about the sub-issue of the opportunities that attracted Scots to other lands.

◆ 'How useful …' questions can be about **either** the main issue **or** one of the sub-issues.

◆ The marker's instructions say: 'The candidate makes a judgement on how useful Source A is as evidence of the opportunities that attracted Scots to other lands, in terms of…'. This tells you that the marker is expecting you to make a **judgement**. Do not miss this out.

◆ The list that follows this gives details of what the marker expects to see in terms of the **origin**, **purpose** and **content** of the source. Note that there are three points of valid content that can be used in answering the question. The points on origin and purpose are prompts for you to explore further these features of the source.

◆ The first set of recalled knowledge points support and develop those in the source. The second put the source in a wider context. Developing points with further detail from the source itself gets the same reward as bringing in new information.

◆ 'Any other relevant factors' is the final point in the marker's list. This allows you to bring in information that may be specific to a particular locality that you have studied or other valid information.

Now that we've seen inside the mind of a Higher History marker, let's apply this knowledge to some example questions.

Read the following source and answer. What mark would you give the answer and why? Think about what you have read and the previous example.

Example

Source B: from William Gallacher, *Revolt on the Clyde* (1936).

> The 'tuppence an hour' strike was over. We were back once more in the factories. But the strike had made a deep political change. Any hope the war-makers might have had of spreading the war fever throughout the Clyde was now gone for ever. The workers knew their enemies, and that they were not across the North Sea. Revolutionary agitators, under McLean's tuition, were increasing in number day by day, and were warmly cheered at mass meetings wherever they went. It became increasingly difficult for the 'patriots' to get a hearing. From the very beginning the Socialists of Glasgow took a firm stand against the war. This was evidenced when Ben Tillett came to fulfil an engagement with the Clarion Scouts. The meeting was in the Pavilion Theatre. Ben shrieked his undying hatred of the Hun, but the audience of Socialists hooted him off the platform.

How useful is **Source B** in explaining the growth of radicalism in politics in Scotland? (5 marks)

In reaching a conclusion you should refer to:

◆ *the origin and possible purpose of the source*

◆ *the content of the source*

◆ *recalled knowledge.*

Example Answer 1

Source B is fairly useful as evidence of the growth of radicalism in Scotland during the period of the First World War. However, as evidence of the growth of radicalism in Scotland, it is only one man's perspective, using one incident, in one city. It misses out many other relevant points which could be used as evidence.

Source B was written by an important figure in the trade union movement in Scotland. Willie Gallacher was involved in the Shop Stewards' movement and founded the Communist Party in Scotland after the war. As such, he is an interesting author if studying the radicalisation of Scottish politics. As the source is clearly his own recollections of trade union activities around the Clyde, its purpose is likely to be very favourable towards radical actions.

The content of Source B does indeed show a radical uprising on the Clyde as the workers demand more pay. However, Gallacher's claim that it caused deep political change and ended the pro-war attitude on the Clyde is perhaps exaggerated, as most workers did see it as their duty to help those on the front line by helping the war effort, and so worked hard. It also mentions the famous revolutionary John McLean, depicting him as a leader and mentor to the

Example answer continued ➤

Example Answer 1 continued)

so-called 'agitators'. In fact, though McLean was inspirational to those who supported him, outright socialists were in a minority, and after being arrested many times, he became a less prominent figure. Lastly, Gallacher says that the Glasgow socialists prevented those they dubbed 'patriots' from speaking and promoting the pro-war cause. However, as already stated, the pro-war spirit stayed strong due to a sense of duty.

On the other hand, Source B does not make any reference to the significance of elections in demonstrating the broader growth of radicalism. For instance, in the 1922 elections, the Independent Labour Party, which consisted of the more left-wing members of the Labour Party, were a huge majority in Glasgow. Out of 43 hopeful Labour MP candidates, 40 belonged to the ILP. These threatened to bring a more socialist agenda if elected. However, this never really came to anything as the minority government formed with the Liberals restricted how radical they could make Scotland.

Overall, Source B is evidence of the growth of radicalism, but more so in Glasgow than in Scotland as a whole, as it really talks about the socialist feeling that sprang up in the factories there.

How good do you think this answer is? What mark did you give it? A marker might make the following comments about the answer.

The candidate has made evaluation directly in terms of the question. There is extended exploration of origin and purpose, as the candidate clearly knows who Willie Gallacher was and his importance. Some comments on purpose are made, which show awareness of a perspective on the past. **(2 marks)**

The source has been effectively interpreted with separate points assessed:

◆ *Radical rising: workers demand more pay; however, the claim that it caused political change and ended pro-war attitudes is commented on.*

◆ *John McLean, leader and mentor: inspirational to those who supported him.*

◆ *Glasgow socialists prevented those they dubbed 'patriots' from speaking.*

Three good points made, but only **2 marks** *given in accordance with the marking instructions.*

Relevant and appropriate recalled knowledge has been applied to the answer. It has been assessed in a skilful way:

◆ *Point about the majority of workers on Clyde doing their duty and helping with the war effort.*

◆ *Point about the development of the ILP in Glasgow and its potential for further radicalising the Labour Party.*

(2 marks)

Nice overall conclusion in terms of the question finishes the response. The candidate does more than enough to gain the full **5 marks**.

Here is a second answer to the question. Now you are the marker. Make a photocopy of the answer and give it marks in the way illustrated above.

Example Answer 2

Source B states that the 'tuppence an hour' strike had made a deep political change and the workers now knew their real enemies, who were not across the seas. The source states that any hope of pro-war fever was gone and McLean (a great Scottish revolutionary) was warmly supported. The number of revolutionary agitators was increasing daily, according to Source B. It also mentions that it became hard for patriots to be heard and pro-war Ben Tillett was booed at a meeting in the Pavilion Theatre. The source fails to mention, however, that most workers supported the war and worked hard, not all participating in strikes. The agitators such as McLean were cheered, but the source fails to mention their long-term impact, which was fairly limited. Source B is fairly useful as evidence of the growth of radicalism. It was written by someone present at the time and shows their viewpoint, although it is biased and misses out major facts.

Questions you might want to ask yourself before marking the answer are these:

◆　Is there a good exploration of the origin and purpose of the source?

◆　How is the information from the source used? Is it merely description, or is it analysed?

◆　How is recalled information linked to the answer? Is this information analysed in terms of the question?

A marker might make the following points regarding this answer.

Judgement in terms of the question appears at the end of the answer, but the exploration of origin and purpose is very poor, so no credit is given for the provenance of the source.

*The source is interpreted, but it is very much listing points from the source. It is a descriptive interpretation, as little is made in the way of analysis. However, the judgement at the end saves this and **1 mark** is given:*

◆　*The 'tuppence an hour' strike made a deep political change; any hope of pro-war fever was gone.*

◆　*McLean was supported; the number of revolutionary agitators was increasing.*

◆　*Pro-war patriots were booed at a meeting in the Pavilion Theatre.*

(1 mark)

A reasonable point is made that is linked in a basic way to help the answer:

◆　*Most workers supported the war and worked hard, so McLean's impact was limited.*

(1 mark)

***2 marks out of 5** are awarded.*

SOURCE COMPARISON QUESTIONS

What is the point of comparing historical sources?

The comparison of views is an important skill for a historian to master. Views about important historical events differ, including views at the time of the event itself. People can agree and disagree about events. If two people watch exactly the same football match and agree about the game, it is likely they support the same side. But if those two people support different sides they are more likely to disagree about events on the pitch. Or you might get two people who agree on some bits of the game, but disagree on others. People in the past were no different to people today. For example, an English chronicler and a Scottish chronicler will probably have very different views about the Battle of Bannockburn. Historians too can differ in their interpretation of events. It is important to develop the skills that can identify these differences.

In the Higher History exam, sources for comparison will relate to one of the general issues or specific sub-issues. Each will contain four points of direct comparison, relating to **causes**, **consequences** or **analysis** of developments.

In order to encourage you to identify the similarities and differences between two sources, the question takes the form: 'To what extent do **Sources A** and **B** agree about … ?'

For the comparison question you will need to explain the extent to which the sources agree about an event or a development. Don't forget to ATQ!

Identifying the level of agreement is **very important** in your answer. This point will be developed below, but it is useful to get the idea in your head now.

Good practice

If you start your answer by saying, 'Sources A and B agree totally/partially/not at all about …', the marker will see that you are making a judgement about the sources. **Remember**, the judgement will change depending on the sources you are given.

Bad practice

If, on the other hand, you start your answer by saying, 'Sources A and B both talk about …', the marker will think: 'Ah ha! There is no judgement here. It looks like description.' You may go on to develop your answer well, but it will not have got off to a good start.

Hints and Tips

Underneath each question in the exam paper there is a prompt to help you. It tells you what the examiners are looking for. For the question 'To what extent do Sources A and B agree about … ?', the prompt is as follows.

◆ *Compare the content overall and in detail.*

How are answers to this question marked?

As with the source evaluation question, the marker has a set of guidelines to help decide how many marks your answer will get. Markers use a grid like the one below as a guide to help them spot and assess what they are looking for.

There are five marks allocated to this question.

Feature of marking	Mark allocation	Marks given	Overall mark
Overall comparison	Up to 2 marks		
Direct comparisons	Up to 4 marks		

As you can see, the number of marks allocated comes to six in all. This means that you can achieve the full five marks in a couple of ways.

Overall comparison

The wording of the question, 'To what extent … ?', tells us that the overall evaluation of the sources is important. Up to two marks are allocated for this feature, so it is worth doing well. You will need to show an awareness of the extent to which the sources agree with each other. As already discussed, a judgement must be made. It is important to back up this judgement with an outline of the content areas where there is agreement or disagreement. If the judgement gives you one mark, then the other mark is given for the quality of your identification of the areas of agreement or disagreement. This has to be based on the content.

The judgement that you come to must be based on the evidence in front of you. Just because the question's wording is about to what extent the sources agree does not mean that they will necessarily agree. You need to be aware that the sources might totally disagree, or there might be points of agreement and disagreement between them. So the agreement might be 'to a certain extent'. It all depends on what is in the source in front of you. This means that **you must react to the evidence**.

Direct comparisons

After the overall evaluation, you are expected to compare content directly on a point-by-point basis. This has to be more than a simple 'A says, but B says/omits'. Some basic explanation of what the two sources agree or disagree about, combined with illustration of the point from the sources, is needed in order for a full mark to be given.

No credit will be given for 'ghost comparisons'! In other words, no credit is given for saying 'A says this, but B does not mention it at all'. Comparison of the **presented content** is what is being assessed, so all of your judgements must be based on the two presented sources. There will be **four** points of comparison between the two sources.

Hints *and* Tips

It is good practice to finish with an overall sentence summing up the answer.

Remember

Here is a useful checklist for answering the comparison question:

◆ Come to a **judgement** about the extent to which the sources agree with each other.

◆ Back up this judgement with an **outline** of the areas of agreement/disagreement.

◆ Identify **individual points** of agreement or difference and show this through the use of **examples** from both sources. These can be as short quotes or in your own words.

◆ Conclude, giving an **overall judgement**.

Read the following sources and answer. What mark would you give the answer and why?

Example

Source A: from F. Mignet, *The History of Mary, Queen of Scots* (1851).

> Mary's actions before and after the murder are quite sufficient to convince us that she was involved in the murder plot. Her journey to Glasgow took place at a time when she was openly expressing her distrust and hatred of Darnley. She showed tenderness towards him and expressed hopes of being reconciled with him in order to persuade him to come with her to Edinburgh. Kirk o' Field was selected as the most convenient place to commit the crime. Mary consented to reside at this house so that Darnley would not refuse to live there. On the evening before the murder she removed from the house all the furniture of any value that it contained.

Example continued ➤

Example continued

Source B: from S. Cowan, *Mary, Queen of Scots and Who Wrote the Casket Letters?* (1907).

Mary went to Glasgow with nothing in her heart but the most loving devotion to her husband. From that time, until his death, any other interpretation of her actions would be inconsistent with the best historical narratives of her life. She nursed him day and night during her visit, after which he proposed that she should take him with her to Edinburgh. She suggested Craigmillar as it was situated on higher ground and very healthy. Curiously enough, he refused to go there. Mary wrote to Maitland to provide a house. Maitland recommended Kirk o' Field, allegedly after showing Bothwell the letter. We think this is very unlikely as Bothwell was in Liddesdale, seventy miles away. It is clear that Maitland was a member of the conspiracy who wanted to put Darnley into Kirk o' Field.

To what extent do **Sources A** and **B** agree about the involvement of Mary, Queen of Scots in the death of Darnley? (5 marks)

◆ *Compare the content overall and in detail.*

Example Answer 1

Sources A and B agree about the involvement of Mary, Queen of Scots in the death of Darnley, but only in a very limited way, as both agree that Darnley was killed in Kirk o' Field. However, the sources mostly differ in that Source A feels Mary had some obvious involvement, while Source B feels that Mary had nothing to do with the murder and instead blames Maitland. The sources disagree about Mary's feelings for Darnley, as Source A states that Mary, 'openly expressed her distrust and hatred of Darnley', in contrast to Source B, which says, 'there was nothing in her heart, but the most loving devotion to her husband.' Both sources therefore disagree about how Mary truly felt towards Darnley. This is further shown as Source A says that Mary showed tenderness to Darnley, but only pretended to reconcile herself with Darnley to persuade him to come with her so that the murder could take place; however, Source B denies that Mary had any involvement, claiming that she nursed him night and day and blames Maitland for arranging Darnley's death. The sources also disagree as to why Kirk o' Field was selected as a place to stay. Source A says that Mary convinced Darnley to return with her and that Kirk o' Field was selected as a convenient place to commit the crime. On the other hand, Source B says that Mary had suggested Craigmillar as a healthy place to stay, but that Maitland recommended Kirk o' Field. Source A very much blames Mary for arranging Darnley's death in 1567. It says that she moved to the house to ensure that Darnley would live there. However, Source B completely disagrees – it does not blame Mary in any way and blames Maitland as 'a member of the conspiracy who wanted to put Darnley into Kirk o' Field.' The sources disagree on Mary's true feelings for Darnley and differ in their views of her involvement in the death of Darnley completely.

How good do you think this answer is? What mark did you give it? A marker might make the following comments about the answer.

*The question is addressed directly in the first two sentences. A judgement as to the extent of agreement about the involvement of Mary, Queen of Scots in the death of Darnley is made and this is further developed with relevant extraction of the areas of similarity and difference. (**2 marks** awarded for the overall comparison.)*

*Four substantive points of comparison can be identified. These are exemplified through content from the sources. Sometimes this is quoted directly and at other times the candidate uses their own words. Both are valid methods of developing the comparison. The first two comparisons exemplify differences about how Mary felt. The third is about why Kirk o' Field was selected as a place to stay. The fourth is the weakest, as there is no overall stem, but there is very strong development of the sources' content to exemplify who was to blame for arranging Darnley's death. (**4 marks** achieved for the individual points of comparison.)*

Points from source:

◆ *The sources disagree about Mary's feelings for Darnley: Source A says that Mary expressed hatred for him; Source B says she was devoted to him.*

◆ *This is further shown as Source A says that Mary showed tenderness to Darnley, but that this was a pretence to persuade him to come with her so that the murder could take place; Source B denies that Mary had any involvement, claiming that she nursed him, and blames Maitland for arranging his death.*

◆ *The sources also disagree as to why Kirk o' Field was selected as a place to stay: Source A says that Mary convinced Darnley to return with her and that Kirk o' Field was selected as a convenient place to commit the crime; Source B says that Mary had suggested Craigmillar as a healthy place to stay, but that Maitland recommended Kirk o' Field.*

◆ *Source A very much blames Mary for arranging Darnley's death in 1567. It says that she moved to the house to ensure that Darnley would live there. However, Source B disagrees: it does not blame Mary but blames Maitland as a conspirator.*

The overall concluding sentence at the end of the answer is not necessary for full marks, but is good practice and provides a tidy end to the answer.

*This answer easily achieves the full **5 marks**.*

Here is a second answer to the question. Now you are the marker. Make a photocopy of the answer and try to apply marks in the way illustrated above.

Example Answer 2

Sources A and B are completely different in their views of Mary. Source A openly accuses her of murdering her husband, Darnley, while Source B is convinced that she was devoted to Darnley and had nothing to do with his demise. Both sources were written within sixty years of each other, and are secondary sources. Source A states that Mary went to Glasgow while feeling hostile to Darnley. Source B states that she went to Glasgow feeling devoted to her husband. Source A sets Mary up as the murderer of Darnley, but Source B is adamant that Maitland was responsible. Source A does not mention that Craigmillar was the first suggestion for where Darnley could stay. However, Source A says that Mary removed all of the valuable furniture from Kirk o' Field on the evening before the murder. Source B neglects to say this.

Here are some questions you might want to ask yourself before marking the answer.

◆ Is there an overall judgement in terms of the question?

◆ Is evidence used to illustrate the extent to which the sources agree with each other?

◆ How is the answer developed? Are comparisons made then illustrated through the content of the presented sources? If not, are the comparison points enough to gain any sort of credit?

A marker might make the following points regarding this answer.

*The first two sentences provide a basic overall comparison, but it is not directly in terms of the posed question. The second sentence illustrates the comparison, and the selection of evidence illustrates an awareness of disagreement between the sources. (**1 mark** awarded for overall comparison.)*

The facts that both sources were written within sixty years of each other, and are secondary sources, are not relevant to the answer, so no credit is awarded.

Some basic comparison points are then made. These are listed rather than explicitly compared, and there is no overall comparison or evidence used to illustrate the point:

◆ *Source A states that Mary went to Glasgow feeling hostile to Darnley. Source B states that she went to Glasgow feeling devoted to her husband.*

◆ *Source A sets Mary up as the murderer of Darnley, but Source B is adamant that Maitland was responsible.*

(**1 mark** awarded)

The rest of the answer is a series of ghost comparisons, for which no credit can be given.

2 marks out of 5 *are awarded.*

PLACING SOURCES IN THEIR HISTORICAL CONTEXT

Why is a historical context important for sources?

A historian needs to place sources in their timeframe. Awareness of the broad events that surround a source is vital if a historian is to be fully informed about events. The questions on the context of a source test your ability to relate a source to your broader knowledge of the period.

These questions will relate to a **general issue** and a **specific sub-issue** from the course content. So there will be **two** questions testing this skill. The wording at the start of the question will tell you which is being assessed.

◆ If a question begins, '**How fully** does Source A … ?', it relates to a **general issue**.

◆ If a question begins, '**How far** does Source B … ?', it relates to a **specific sub-issue**. There are **three** sub-issues within each of the four general issues.

Although the skill being assessed is the same for both questions, the level of detail required in the answers does differ. The '**How fully**' question is far more general than the '**How far**' question, which will need much more specific knowledge.

For **both** the 'How fully' and 'How far' questions you will need to come to a judgement about how far or how fully the sources explain events or developments from the subject you have studied. Don't forget to ATQ!

Unlike the 'How useful' question, these questions do **NOT** require you to comment on origin and purpose. **However**, they do have one thing in common with the 'How useful' question. The source or sources presented will only give you part of the picture (remember, historians write complete books to explain developments and events), so a source is only going to be able to tell you part of the answer. You will need to show that you have identified information that the source does not include, but which is needed for a full answer to the question.

First let's look at how questions are created. This can help focus your revision if you know the types of question that will be asked.

The table on page 58 shows an example from Special Topic 2: The Age of Reformation, 1542–1603. It shows for each topic area the main issue, an example of the question asked about the main issue, the three sub-issues and the example questions asked about them.

WHAT CONTENT IS RELEVANT ? WHAT IS NOT MENTIONED IN THE SOURCE ?

SOURCE

Main issue	1. The Reformation of 1560
Question on main issue	How fully does Source A illustrate the reasons for the Reformation of 1560?
Content	The nature of the church in Scotland; attempts at reform; the growth of Protestantism; relationships with France and England; religious conflict; Lords of the Congregation; Treaty of Edinburgh, 1560
Questions on sub-issues	How far does Source B show the weaknesses of the Catholic Church in Scotland?
	How far does Source C illustrate the growth of Protestantism?
	How far does Source D explain the influence of England and/or France on religious developments in Scotland?
Main issue	**2. The reign of Mary, 1561–1567**
Question on main issue	How fully does Source A explain the reasons for Mary's loss of her throne?
Content	Mary's difficulties in ruling Scotland: religion; gender; relations with the nobility; Mary's marriages; her relationship with England; abdication; flight to England
Questions on sub-issues	How far does Source B illustrate Mary's difficulties in ruling Scotland?
	How far does Source C give evidence of Mary's relationship with England?
	How far does Source D show the contribution Mary, Queen of Scots made to the loss of her throne?
Main issue	**3. James VI and the relationship between monarch and Kirk**
Question on main issue	How fully does Source A illustrate the relationship between monarch and Kirk in the reign of James VI?
Content	The struggle for control of the Kirk; from regency to personal rule; differing views about the roles of the monarch and the Kirk
Questions on sub-issues	How far does Source B show the efforts of James VI to control the Kirk?
	How far does Source C illustrate the efforts of the Kirk to maintain its independence?
	How far does Source D indicate the outcome of the attempts of James VI to control the Kirk by 1603?
Main issue	**4. The impact of the Reformation on Scotland, to 1603**
Question on main issue	How fully does Source A show the impact of the Reformation on Scotland?
Content	The social, cultural, educational and economic impact of the Reformation on Scotland, to 1603
Questions on sub-issues	How far does Source B illustrate the social impact of the Reformation on Scotland, to 1603?
	How far does Source C show the cultural impact of the Reformation on Scotland, to 1603?
	How far does Source D explain the economic impact of the Reformation on Scotland, to 1603?

As we have already mentioned, an answer to a 'How fully' or 'How far' question must include a judgement. Don't forget to include one! We will develop this point later on.

Hints and Tips

Underneath each question in this part of the exam paper there is a prompt to help you. It tells you what the examiners are looking for. For the 'How fully' and 'How far' questions, the prompt is as follows.

◆ *Use the source and recalled knowledge.*

How are answers to this question marked?

Markers may use a grid like the one below when allocating marks. It gives a good guide on what to look for.

The question will be worded as follows: 'How fully/far does **Source A** explain/illustrate/ show…?'

There will be ten marks allocated to each of these questions.

Feature of marking	Mark allocation	Marks given	Overall mark
Use of source	Up to 4 marks		
Use of relevant recalled knowledge	Up to 7 marks		

The source will contain four separate points relevant to the answer. It may also contain information that is not relevant. Be careful this doesn't distract you! Make sure you **read the question** carefully.

You will notice that the total number of marks adds up to eleven. This means you can achieve full marks in a couple of ways. If you can only identify three points from the source you can gain full marks with a full seven recalled points. Similarly, if you identify four points from the source you only need to provide six recalled points to achieve full marks. The marks for each of the features are achieved in the following ways.

Judgement

You need to make a **judgement** about how far or how fully the source explains/illustrates/ shows a cause, characteristics or consequences of an event.

Remember the advice we gave in previous questions about starting your answer with an evaluation that answers the question. You need to do exactly the same here and remember that the presented source or sources will **NOT** be enough – they will not explain a development fully enough or far enough. **You must make a judgement!**

Use of source

You can gain up to four marks for **interpretation** of the parts of the source that are **relevant**, in terms of the question. For full marks to be given, you need to comment on points **in terms of the question**. Merely selecting relevant information and/or listing is only worth one point.

Use of relevant recalled knowledge

You will earn your remaining marks, up to a maximum of seven, by providing relevant and developed **recalled knowledge**. This can be either points of extended development from the source content or new, but relevant, information. This has to be developed **in terms of the question** for full marks to be given.

Hints *and* Tips

As with the other kinds of source questions, it is good practice to finish with an overall sentence summing up the answer.

Remember

Here is a useful checklist for answering the questions about the context of sources:

◆ Come to a **judgement** as to how fully/far the source explains the causes, characteristics or consequences of an event in terms of the overall question.

◆ Identify the main **relevant points** made in the source and **comment** on these.

◆ Identify areas that **extend** the points in the source or that are not mentioned in the source, but that relate to the question.

◆ Conclude, giving an **overall judgement**.

The 'How fully ... ?' source context question

Remember that this question needs broad knowledge of the overall issue being assessed. This example is taken from Special Topic 1, on the Scottish Wars of Independence. It looks at Issue 3, on Scottish resistance to Edward I of England, 1296–1305.

Example 1

Source A: from the Chronicle of Walter of Guisborough, 1297.

> The earl of Warenne, to whom our king had committed the care and custody of the whole kingdom of Scotland, said he could not stay there and keep his health. He stayed in England and sluggishly pursued the enemy. A public robber called William Wallace, a

Example 1 continued ➤

Example 1 *continued*

vagrant fugitive, called all the exiles to himself and made himself almost their prince; they grew to be numerous. With him was associated also William Douglas, who at the taking of the castle of Berwick had surrendered himself and his men to our king, saving his life and limb. When the king had restored him he became unmindful of these good deeds and turned robber working with a robber. The two Williams with perverse people thought they could find the justiciar of our king at Scone, where he had heard pleas, and they hastened to destroy him. But he was forewarned and escaped with difficulty, leaving to the enemy many spoils.

How fully does **Source A** illustrate Scottish resistance to Edward I between 1296 and 1305? (10 marks)

◆ *Use the source and recalled knowledge.*

Example Answer 1

Source A illustrates the Scottish resistance to Edward between 1296 and 1305, but only to a limited extent. It illustrates the beginnings of the resistance, but fails to look at the events after 1297. The source mentions the emergence of William Wallace as a leader of the rebellion, but from an English point of view, as it describes him as 'a public robber called William Wallace, a vagrant fugitive', who drew exiles to him and they grew numerous. Wallace was considered to be an outsider by most of the traditional Scottish nobility and they were slow to join him.

On the other hand, the source also mentions the role of William Douglas, who was clearly seen by the chronicler as a traitor, but who had turned against Edward and worked 'with a robber'. Douglas had led the Scottish garrison at Berwick when it had been sacked by Edward I's army. He had surrendered, but was the first Scottish nobleman to join with Wallace when he rebelled. The source also mentions these two leaders taking action against Edward's representatives in Scotland by searching for the justiciar of the king to destroy him. It also mentions that he fled and left many 'spoils' for the triumphant Scots. This was true of the beginning of the Scottish resistance. The English were arrogant in their rule of Scotland and were surprised by the strength of Scottish resistance and fled. This led to a number of English invasions which were never successful until 1304–05.

However, the source does not mention the wide nature of the resistance. Andrew Moray rebelled in the north and joined forces with Wallace to push the English out of Scotland. It also fails to mention the magnificent victory of the Scottish army at Stirling Bridge over the English, killing the hated Hugh de Cressingham. He was so hated that the Scots made a scabbard out of his skin. The victory also led to the death of Andrew Moray, which was a blow to the Scots, but resistance continued and was largely successful until the defeat at Falkirk. Wallace dropped out of view at this time and on his return was betrayed and executed by Edward I. This was not the end of Scottish resistance, however. The Bruce and Comyn families continued the struggle against Edward until 1305.

Source A shows us the beginnings of Scottish resistance to Edward, but fails to give information on what happened later.

How good do you think this answer is? What mark did you give it? A marker might make the following comments about the answer.

There is some decent overall judgement as to how fully the source illustrates Scottish resistance at the beginning of the answer. The answer ends with a single sentence giving an overall conclusion in terms of the question.

The source is assessed reasonably well, with good use of the first two points in particular.

Points from the source:

◆ *The emergence of William Wallace as a leader of the rebellion, but from an English point of view, as it describes him as 'a public robber called William Wallace, a vagrant fugitive', who drew exiles to him and they grew numerous.*

◆ *The role of William Douglas, who was clearly seen by the chronicler as a traitor, but who had turned against Edward and worked 'with a robber'.*

◆ *The source also mentions these two leaders taking action against Edward's representatives in Scotland by searching for the justiciar of the king to destroy him.*

◆ *It also mentions that he fled and left many 'spoils' for the triumphant Scots.*

(4 marks)

Extension of points from the source are well made and add to the answer:

◆ *Wallace was considered to be an outsider by most of the traditional Scottish nobility and they were slow to join him. Douglas was the first noble to join the rebellion.*

◆ *The English were surprised by the strength of Scottish resistance and were pushed out of Scotland, leading to numerous English invasions, which were not successful until 1304–05.*

(2 marks)

Broader recall is well structured and makes a number of good points:

◆ *However, the source does not mention the wide nature of the resistance. Andrew Moray rebelled in the north and joined forces with Wallace to push the English out of Scotland.*

◆ *It also fails to mention the magnificent victory of the Scottish army at Stirling Bridge over the English.*

◆ *The victory also led to the death of Andrew Moray, which was a blow to the Scots, but resistance continued and was largely successful until the defeat at Falkirk.*

◆ *Wallace dropped out of view at this time and on his return was betrayed and executed by Edward I.*

◆ *This was not the end of Scottish resistance, however. The Bruce and Comyn families continued the struggle against Edward until 1305.*

(5 possible marks)

10 out of 10 marks

Hints and Tips

To help you see how a good answer is structured, make a photocopy of this answer and take three highlighter pens. Use one colour to highlight points taken from the source, then use another to identify points extending the source information. Next, use another colour to identify the new information being used.

 Again, this question needs broad knowledge of the overall issue being assessed. This example is taken from Special Topic 5, on the impact of the Great War on Scotland. It looks at Issue 2, on the domestic impact of the war on Scottish society and culture.

Example 2

Source B: a photograph of a rent strike demonstration in Glasgow in 1915.

How fully does Source B show the impact of the war on Scottish society? (10 marks)

◆ *Use the source and recalled knowledge.*

Example Answer 2

Source B shows us one of the main ways in which the First World War had an impact on Scottish society. It shows us a demonstration against rent rises in Glasgow in 1915. This makes it a primary source. Landlords took advantage of increased demand for rented property in cities like Glasgow and Dundee to put up rents. This caused demonstrations like the one above, where local communities, often led by women, rose up to 'defend our homes against Landlord Tyranny', as one of the posters says. Women like Mary Barbour and Helen Crawfurd in Glasgow led the rent strikes and stopped the bailiffs sent by the courts when they tried to evict people from their flats. They led rent strikes, which is also shown in the source by two posters calling for rent strikes saying that they are not for removing. The rent strikes were very effective and eventually the Government was forced to pass a Rent Restriction Act. This froze the level of rent paid. The campaigns were very emotional, as the source shows, with children pushed to the front complaining that while their daddy was away fighting, people at home were also fighting Huns, which means the landlords.

Although the source shows one major effect of the war on Scottish society, the war had a much wider impact. The Defence of the Realm Act put a lot of restrictions on what people could do. It forced people to work in particular jobs and it allowed the Government to restrict the opening hours of pubs, for example. Many Scots went and fought on the Western Front. Because they fought well, many Scots were also killed, which had a big effect on Scottish societies. This can be seen in the memorials in every town and village in Scotland. There is a big national war memorial in Edinburgh Castle to remember those who fell. Therefore, though Source B shows one major effect of the war it does not show it all.

How good do you think this answer is? Have a go at marking it yourself.

Key Points

◆ Has a judgement been made in terms of the question?
◆ Has the source been interpreted effectively? How many points have been made from the source?
◆ Is the information from the source balanced by information from recalled knowledge?

Decide how many marks you would give the answer and say why you have given these marks.

The 'How far … ?' source context question

As in the 'How fully' questions, this question needs specific knowledge of the sub-issue being assessed. This example is taken from Special Topic 2: The Age of Reformation, 1542–1603. It is from the sub-issue about the weaknesses of the Catholic Church in Scotland. This is from the first main issue, on the reasons for the Reformation of 1560 in Scotland.

Example 1

Source C: from Keith Brown, *Reformation to Union, 1560–1707*, ed. Houston and Knox (2001).

> The pre-Reformation Roman Catholic Church in Scotland was certainly not wholly corrupt, nor had it entirely lost the trust and confidence of all the Scottish people. Pockets of real spirituality existed in the monasteries, there were priests who laboured hard in their parishes and good works were evident in the hospices and in alms-giving. On the other hand, a robust, vibrant, self-confident church would not have been swept away so easily in 1560. Abandoned by its bishops, undefended by an often ill-educated clergy with low morale, and earning little respect from a laity that was angered by abuses within the church and enthused by the fresh ideas emanating from Protestant Europe, Scottish Catholicism collapsed almost immediately as the protection of French military force was removed.

How far does **Source C** explain the weaknesses of the Catholic Church in Scotland before the Reformation of 1560? (10 marks)

◆   *Use the source and recalled knowledge.*

Example Answer 1

Many problems faced the Catholic Church before the Reformation of 1560. Source C explains some of these problems well, but it fails to give us the whole picture. The source mentions that there was still strength in the Catholic Church, in particular in the monasteries, but the reality was that monastic life was in decline in Scotland, and this did not help the Catholic Church, as it added to the idea that it had lost touch with the people. The source refers to the fact that the laity were angered by abuses within the church. This was true, as ordinary people saw their contributions to the church being taken from their local parish by the bishops and abbots. This made them rich.

It is clear from the source that the church was in a bad way, as it talks about the clergy not defending it, as they were not well educated and had low morale. This is true – not all priests were able to preach since they could not read. As a result they did not know the message from the Bible and Catholic beliefs. Added to this was the fact that many priests had illegitimate children who even inherited parishes from their fathers. This did not look good for the Catholic Church, which is why it was replaced by Protestant beliefs.

Source C tells us a lot about the weaknesses and problems the Catholic Church faced in Scotland, but does not go into detail about them in any way.

How good do you think this answer is? What mark did you give it? A marker might make the following comments about the answer.

This is an interesting answer, because the source has a lot of distracting information about the strengths of the Catholic Church at the beginning. There is a clear attempt to make a judgement in terms of the question, even if it is a little limited. This can be seen at the beginning and at the end. The candidate is clearly trying to answer the question.

Points from the source (these are fairly limited and one is irrelevant, but is linked to relevant recalled knowledge):

◆ *The source mentions that there was still strength in the Catholic Church: no credit for this.*

◆ *The source refers to the fact that the laity were angered by abuses within the church.*

◆ *It is clear from the source that the church was in a bad way as it talks about the clergy not defending it, as they were not well educated and had low morale.*

(2 marks)

Extension of points through recalled knowledge (most of the recalled knowledge here extends and gives examples from what has been mentioned in the source):

◆ *The reality was that monastic life was in decline in Scotland, and this did not help the Catholic Church, as it added to the idea that it had lost touch with the people.*

◆ *Ordinary people saw their contributions to the church being taken from their local parish by the bishops and abbots. This made them rich.*

◆ *Not all priests were able to preach since they could not read. As a result they did not know the message from the Bible and Catholic beliefs.*

◆ *Many priests had illegitimate children who even inherited parishes from their fathers. This did not look good for the Catholic Church, which is why it was replaced by Protestant beliefs.*

(4 marks)

*Overall **6 marks out of 10**. It is a decent answer, but has not been extended enough by use of the source or more recalled knowledge.*

How do you think you could improve this answer? For example, are there any points you can identify in the source that might be included?

Again, this question needs specific knowledge of the sub-issue being assessed. This example is taken from Special Topic 3: The Treaty of Union, 1689–1740. It is from the sub-issue about the economic effects of the Union to 1740. This is from the fourth main issue, on the effects of the Union to 1740.

Example 2

Source D: from Christopher Whatley, *Scottish Society 1707–1830* (2000).

Some small but significant changes in trading patterns produced temporary dislocation. Being bound by British commercial policy meant that long-standing Scottish trade links with France and the Low Countries were weakened. Imports of popular French claret, for example, had to be replaced by legal traders with heavier, sweeter wine from England's ally, Portugal, and indeed the largest single contribution to the post-1707 increase in shipping activity came from voyages to and from Spain and Portugal. The number of ships

Example 2 continued ➤

Example 2 continued

from England rose too, as did other forms of coastal trading. According to contemporaries, but overlooked by most historians, the immediate beneficiaries of Union were the landowners and merchants who engaged in the seaborne grain trade. The impact is striking, with grain and oatmeal shipments from Scotland more than doubling.

How far does **Source D** explain the economic effects of Union to 1740? (10 marks)

◆ *Use the source and recalled knowledge.*

Example Answer 2

Source D shows that the Union with England had a number of economic effects on Scotland. The source shows that the Union meant that Scotland traded with different countries. Her old trading partners like France and the Low Countries were replaced by products and trade with Portugal and Spain, who were England's friends. It also tells us that people who benefited from the Union were landowners and merchants who sold grain. Trade in grain and oatmeal more than doubled, according to the source.

Most Scots did not benefit from the Union at all. Trades like the Scottish linen trade suffered compared to the English woollen trade. Also it took a long time for Scotland to get used to English taxes. English taxes were higher than those in Scotland. When they were imposed on Scotland there were riots. The Union was not popular with most people in Scotland and they did not like what happened to the Scottish economy.

How good do you think this answer is? What mark did you give it? A marker might make the following comments about the answer.

The answer looks a little brief and, looking at it in detail, it is clear that there are deficiencies. There is no clear evaluation in terms of the question. Recalled knowledge is not linked to the question, and the use of the presented source is largely descriptive. Although the detail in the answer is correctly selected, it will not achieve a pass.

Points from source can be credited as they are appropriate to answer the question, but they are not linked directly to the question. The answer merely states where they have come from:

◆ *The Union meant that Scotland traded with different countries. Her old trading partners like France and the Low Countries were replaced by products and trade with Portugal and Spain, who were England's friends.*

◆ *People who benefited from the Union were landowners and merchants who sold grain. Trade in grain and oatmeal more than doubled, according to the source.*

(2 marks)

Recalled information is described, but it is not linked directly to the question. Again, it is perfectly accurate information, but the evaluation is implicit rather than explicit:

◆ *Most Scots did not benefit from the Union at all. Trades like the Scottish linen trade suffered compared to the English woollen trade.*

◆ *Also it took a long time for Scotland to get used to English taxes. English taxes were higher than those in Scotland. When they were imposed on Scotland there were riots.*

(2 marks)

There is irrelevance at the end, with the statement that the Union was not popular with most people in Scotland and they did not like what happened to the Scottish economy.

4 out of 10 is achieved.

Hints and Tips

In the exam hall:

◆ You have studied hard.

◆ You have learned the facts.

◆ You now need to do the job in the exam.

You have 1 hour and 25 minutes to answer four questions, but remember:

◆ You will need time to read and understand the sources and identify the important information.

◆ You will need time to think about how to structure your answers.

The good news is that you have got quite a lot of time to play with, so make sure your work is the best it can be.

If we include reading time in your allocation for each question, you should think about the following:

◆ The 'How useful' question will take approximately 15 minutes.

◆ The comparison question will take approximately 20 minutes (remember there are two sources here so more reading time is needed!).

◆ The 'How fully'/'How far' questions will take approximately 25 minutes each (remember you need a lot of recall for these and want to make good points with the evidence you have!).

In the end you will work out a system that suits **you**, but above all: **keep an eye on the time**. You do not want to find yourself hurrying the last question.

Good luck in your final exam and remember...

The person who is marking your exam paper wants to see particular things in your answer. Here are two general 'dos':

◆ Do answer the question. Remember to make that **judgement** in terms of the question that is being asked. This is vital for success. The judgement can appear anywhere, but it is

Hints and *Tips* continued ➤

Hints and *Tips continued*

good practice to start with it and use it as a brief conclusion to remind the marker what your line of argument is.

◆ Do select information from the presented sources that is **relevant** to your answer. Ignore material that is not relevant. Make sure you are not just listing information. Where possible comment on it.

And now for some specifics:

◆ Do comment on the **origin** and **purpose** of the source in the 'How useful … ?' question.

◆ Do make the comparison and then **illustrate** it with information from the two presented sources.

◆ Do use relevant **recalled knowledge** to extend points from the presented information in all answers (except for the comparison question).

◆ Do use recalled information to identify events and information that the presented sources **do not cover**.

And here are a couple of things to avoid!

◆ Don't just **describe** the source material.

◆ Don't select **irrelevant** information from the source or from recalled knowledge.

PRACTISE YOUR SOURCE QUESTION SKILLS

In this final part of Section 2 there are questions covering each of the different question types. They are here for you to practise your skills. You can do a number of things with them.

1   You could try to write an answer to the questions in timed circumstances to see how you would get on under examination conditions.

2   You could make up your own marking scheme for each of the questions. Identify the significant views in the source that relate to the question and then think about other information that develops the points from the source as well as new information not covered in the source.

3   Why not think about how you would teach your classmates to answer the question? What are the important parts of the source that you should use? How will you comment on the source content in terms of the question?

4   Each source relates to one of the four main issues for each special topic. Can you identify the issue for your subject?

Suggested approaches to answering the questions are available at www.hoddereducation.co.uk/htphigherhistory.

The 'How useful…' question

Example

Source A is from the *Lanercost Chronicle* describing how Andrew Harclar, Earl of Carlisle, came to an agreement with Robert Bruce in January 1323.

> Now when the Earl of Carlisle heard that the king was at York, he directed his march towards it in order to attack the Scots and drive them out of the kingdom; but when he found the king all in confusion and no army mustered, he disbanded his own forces, allowing every man to return home. The Scots returned laden with spoil and with many prisoners and much booty; and on 1 November they entered Scotland, after remaining in England one month and three days. Wherefore, when the Earl of Carlisle saw that the King of England neither knew how to rule his realm nor was able to defend it against the Scots, who year by year laid it more and more waste, he feared lest at last he [the king] should lose the entire kingdom; so he chose the lesser of two evils, and on 3 January [1323] the Earl of Carlisle went secretly to Robert Bruce at Lochmaben and, after holding long conference and protracted discussion with him, at length came to agreement with him which led to his own destruction.

Example continued ➢

Example continued

How useful is **Source A** in explaining the reasons for the ultimate success of Bruce in maintaining Scotland's independence? (5 marks)

In reaching a conclusion you should refer to:

◆ *the origin and possible purpose of the source*
◆ *the content of the source*
◆ *recalled knowledge.*

Example

Source B is from Reverend Alexander McIvor, Minister for the parish of Sleat, Skye, in the *New Statistical Account of Scotland*, 1834–45.

> The able-bodied among them, after their potatoes are planted in the end of spring, go to the south in search of employment. They return again and their earnings go to pay the landlord's rents. The winter is almost altogether spent in idleness. There is no demand for labour in the parish, and hence there is only occasional exertion on the part of the people. Their food consists principally of potatoes. Oatmeal is a luxury among them, and butcher-meat is seldom tasted. Their poverty arises very much from over-population. There are 225 families in the parish who pay no rents, deriving their subsistence from small portions of land given them by the rent-payers for raising potatoes. These are a burden to the proprietor, inasmuch as they destroy the land in cutting fuel and turn; and are a grievous burden to the inhabitants generally. Their abject poverty stands in the way of any stimulus that may be applied for enabling them to better their condition. The most efficient remedy appears to be an extensive and well regulated emigration.

How useful is **Source B** in showing the factors that forced Scots to leave Scotland? (5 marks)

In reaching a conclusion you should refer to:

◆ *the origin and possible purpose of the source*
◆ *the content of the source*
◆ *recalled knowledge.*

Example

Source **C** is a recruitment poster produced by the British Government in 1915.

How useful is **Source C** for explaining why so many Scots volunteered to fight in the Great War? (5 marks)

In reaching a conclusion you should refer to:

◆ *the origin and possible purpose of the source*

◆ *the content of the source*

◆ *recalled knowledge.*

The comparison question

Example

Source **A** is from the Chronicle of Walter of Guisborough, 1297, describing Wallace's rising in May 1297.

> A public robber called William Wallace, a vagrant fugitive, called all the exiles to himself and made himself almost their prince; they grew to be numerous. With him was associated also Sir William Douglas […]. The two Williams thought they could find the justiciar of our king at Scone … and they hastened to destroy him. But he was forewarned and escaped with difficulty, leaving to the enemy many spoils. They went on no longer secretly confining at the point of the sword all the English whom they could find beyond the sea of Scotland [reference to the River Forth]. Robert Bruce the younger, Earl of Carrick, swore that he would faithfully help our king and his men against the Scots. But he [Bruce] indeed aspiring to the kingdom, instead joined a perverse people, and was allied with the bishop of Glasgow and Steward of Scotland who were the authors of the whole evil. From then on that wicked race and faithless Scots killed all the English whom they could find.

Example *continued* ➤

Example continued

Source B is from Michael Lynch: *Scotland: a new history* (1991).

Although details of the origins of the revolt of 1297 have long been known, the idea persists that Wallace led an uprising of landless peasants. English chroniclers, however, were firm in their suspicions. The real leaders of the revolt, two of them declared, were the ex-Guardians, Robert Wishart, Bishop of Glasgow, and James the Steward, who was Wallace's lord. They were joined shortly after by MacDuff, son of an Earl of Fife, and Bruce, the young Earl of Carrick, who had promised to help Edward, according to the chroniclers. The first outbreaks had taken place in the north rather than in Wallace's territory. The leader of the northern rising was Andrew Murray, the son of a leading baron. Their respective roles in the revolt have been obscured by the fact that Murray died in November 1297, probably of wounds sustained at the battle of Stirling Bridge. Neither a general nor a guerrilla by instinct, Wallace nonetheless deserves to be remembered as an unflinching patriot and a charismatic warlord.

To what extent do **Sources A** and **B** agree about the growth of Scottish resistance to Edward I by 1297? (5 marks)

◆ *Compare the sources overall and in detail.*

Example

Source C is from Martin J Mitchell, *Irish Catholics in the West of Scotland* (2008).

Irish workers were heavily involved in the growth of trade unions of unskilled workers in the late nineteenth century. In 1889 the National Union of Dock Labourers was founded by two Irishmen, Richard McGhee and Edward McHugh. According to Kenefick, dockers in Glasgow were 'overwhelmingly Catholic Irish in composition'. Indeed, what is noticeable is that there was comparatively little open popular hostility to the immigrant presence. Not only did many Irish Catholics mix and associate with Scottish Protestants – a considerable number also married them. It is now apparent that by the end of the nineteenth century the issue of mixed marriages was one which greatly vexed the Catholic Church. It has been suggested that as the century progressed the Catholic Church developed institutions and organisations which locked Catholics into an isolated, self-contained 'cradle to grave' community.

Source D is from J Foster, M Houston and C Madigan, 'Sectarianism, Segregation and Politics on Clydeside in the Later Nineteenth Century', in Martin J Mitchell (ed.) *New Perspectives on the Irish in Scotland* (2008).

Our conclusion was that job discrimination on Clydeside did not operate on a sectarian or religious basis. If there was any discrimination, it tended to operate against all Irish immigrants equally. Where there were exceptions, they appear to have been generated by the Irish themselves. Once on Clydeside there were attempts to introduce Belfast-style

Example continued >

Example continued

patterns of exclusion by monopolising certain unskilled workplaces. Lobban found that in Greenock Protestant immigrants tried to control access to labouring jobs in the cotton mills and refineries; Catholics tried to control labouring work in the docks. This did not work in Glasgow because unskilled workers – including Irish immigrants –were forming trade unions in the late 1880s. In terms of family size, the Protestant and Catholic Irish in Govan and Kinning Park were identical – but the great bulk of men from both religions were married to women born in Ireland.

To what extent do **Sources C** and **D** agree about the experience of Irish immigrants in Scotland? (5 marks)

◆   *Compare the sources overall and in detail.*

Example

Source E is by Grace Kennedy, quoted in *Voices from War* (edited by Ian MacDougall, 1995).

During the war years there was people getting put out of their homes because they couldn't pay their rent. A lot of their men were in the Forces and at that time the soldiers' allowance was a shilling a day and they got half pay. Well, the women got together and we decided that not one soldier's wife would be put out of her home. And guided by Baillie Mary Barbour, who was a plodder and who did tremendous work – we picketed these homes. They barricaded themselves up and we picketed the homes. Then later on there was the Rent Strike. The landlords decided to put the rent up and they did get a 47½ percent increase, which was supposed to be for repairs. Then we had nine months of a Rent Strike. Well, quite a lot got into difficulties through the Rent Strike – financial difficulties. But then the Rent Restriction Act was brought in and I think it was due to the work of Baillie Mary Barbour particularly and the women that the Rent Restriction Act was brought into being.

Source F is from Richard Finlay, *Modern Scotland, 1914–2000* (2004).

It should come as no surprise to find that women were particularly active in the rent strike and in the political agitation surrounding the Clyde. Given the pressures of inflation and the expectation that women were responsible for the household, many felt that direct action was necessary. Women were foremost in the campaign to create a £1 weekly allowance for soldiers' dependents and widows. Women were active in the ranks of the co-operative

Example continued ➤

Example *continued*

movement and the ILP. They were responsible for organising communities to fight the threat of eviction. In the closes and wynds of the local streets and on the factory floor, politics and social and economic grievances became part of everyday conversation. The effect of the Rent Restrictions Act and the campaigns for higher wages and the defence of standards of living arguably made politics more important to women, especially as they were the ones left at home to fight for these causes.

To what extent do **Sources E** and **F** agree about the impact of the war on Scottish women? (5 marks)

◆ *Compare the sources overall and in detail.*

The 'How fully …' question

Example

Source A is from The Macduff case, 1293–5, Record of the King's Bench, November 1293–5.

November 1293: Macduff demands judgement on the king of Scotland as on one with no defence for he is present in the king's court by virtue of an adjournment given to him by the king's writ which he acknowledges that he has received. And upon this it is said to the king of Scotland by his lord the king of England that the king of Scotland is his liegeman for the realm of Scotland for which he performed homage and fealty to him and he has been given an adjournment to appear here before him so that he may answer or say why he will not or should not answer before him.

Afterwards the king of Scotland came before the king and his council and made a personal request of the king: 'Sire I am your liegeman for the realm of Scotland and I pray you to suspend this matter about which you have informed me which affects the people of my realm as well as myself, until I have spoken with them and when I have taken counsel with them I will report to you at your first parliament after Easter.' And the lord king after taking counsel granted the king of Scotland his petition and assigned him a day to appear at the parliament after Easter. The same day was assigned to Macduff.

How fully does **Source A** illustrate the relationship between King John and Edward I? (10 marks)

◆ *Use the source and recalled knowledge.*

Example

Source B is from Ian Whyte, *Scotland before the Industrial Revolution* (1995).

On a longer term view a case can be made for the Union having provided the foundation for Scottish economic growth during the eighteenth century. As well as giving access to English and colonial markets it provided political stability, diminishing the likelihood of Anglo–Scottish conflict. It assured the political and religious settlements of the Revolution of 1688. It allowed easier flow of capital, skills, technology and ideas northwards to combine with Scottish mineral wealth and cheap labour. It is hard to assess the impact on trade as after 1707 goods sent to England for internal consumption were no longer exports and were not recorded but the greatest benefit of the Union was undoubtedly the opening up of English markets. Less tangibly, greater contact with England after 1707 encouraged a fashion for improvement.

How fully does **Source B** explain the effects of the Union, up to 1740? (10 marks)

◆　*Use the source and recalled knowledge.*

Example

Source C is from Allan Macinnes, Marjory Harper and Linda Fryer (eds), *Scotland and the Americas, c.1650–c.1939* (2002).

A significant minority of Scots not only achieved personal success in Canada, but played a key part in shaping the country's development, as explorers, financiers and politicians. Sir John A. Macdonald – the product of a relatively humble home in Glasgow – was five years old when he emigrated with his parents to Kingston, Ontario. He subsequently became a lawyer, and went into politics, initially as an opponent of the colonial government in 1847. Conscious of the ever-present threat from Canada's more powerful neighbour to the south, and totally opposed to separation from Britain, Macdonald's strategy as first Prime Minister of the new Dominion was to promote a transcontinental railway which would join the Atlantic to the Pacific, open up the west to settlers, and in the process strengthen and unite the fledgling country.

How fully does **Source C** describe the impact of Scots emigrants on the Empire? (10 marks)

◆　*Use the source and recalled knowledge.*

The 'How far...' question

Example

Source A is from Fiona Watson, *Under the Hammer: Edward I and Scotland 1286–1307* (1998).

In the aftermath of the Maid's death, Edward certainly maintained an interest in the turn that events might take in the northern kingdom since both the claimants, Robert Bruce and John Balliol, were English landholders. However, the king also recognised that this new situation, although marking the closure of one door, could open up another. To that end, Edward now seized the initiative, summoning the Scots to a parliament to be held at Norham on 6 May 1291.

A small group of Scots crossed the Tweed on 10 May. This deputation was treated to an extraordinary exposition from Edward through the mouth of Roger Brabazon. Though its main thrust related to the king's desire to see the situation justly settled, it also contained two extremely important elements. The first was the most obvious: a demand for both assent to and recognition of, Edward's overlordship as the background to his settlement of the succession. The second was a hint, for the first time, that the settlement was more than a simple adjudication between Bruce and Balliol.

How far does **Source A** illustrate the problems caused by the death of Alexander III? (10 marks)

◆ *Use the source and recalled knowledge.*

Example

Source B is from James Kirk, *Patterns of Reform* (1989).

Protestantism had secured a firm foundation in the politically assertive and progressive areas of Scotland for over a generation before the Reformation parliament in 1560 finally acknowledged the nature of the religious upheaval by intervening to reject papal authority, prohibit the mass and recognise a reformed Confession of Faith. Succeeding waves of Lutheran and Calvinist literature and preaching, fortified by English propaganda, had struck a responsive chord over the decades not merely among intellectual elites of clerics, scholars and the literate but among a remarkable section of the population in town and countryside; who were attracted by reading and discussing, by the power of preaching and psalm singing and by acts of defiance. Discussion of the message of the Reformation occurred not just in isolated house 'cells' by families and friends or in the numerous conventicles in the fields, but increasingly in the market place, at fairs, in taverns and at work: the activism displayed by the craftsmen in Perth in support of the Reformation seems to indicate that religious issues were aired within the context of the workplace.

How far does **Source B** explain the growth of Protestantism in Scotland? (10 marks)

◆ *Use the source and recalled knowledge.*

Example

Source C is from a memoir by Major-General Richard Hilton, a Forward Observation Officer at the battle of Loos, 1915.

> A great deal of nonsense has been written about Loos. The real tragedy of that battle was its nearness to complete success. Most of us who reached the crest of Hill 70 and survived were firmly convinced that we had broken through on that Sunday, 25th September 1915. There seemed to be nothing ahead of us but an unoccupied and incomplete trench system. The only two things that prevented our advancing into the suburbs of Lens were, firstly the exhaustion of the 'Jocks' themselves (for they had undergone a bellyful of marching and fighting that day) and secondly the flanking fire of numerous German machine-guns, which swept that bare hill from some factory buildings in Cite St. Auguste to the south of us. All that we needed was more artillery ammunition to blast those clearly located machine-guns, and some fresh infantry to take over from the weary and depleted 'Jocks' who had done a magnificent job thus far. But, alas, neither ammunition nor reinforcements were immediately available, and the great opportunity passed.

How far does **Source C** illustrate the contribution of the Scots to the military effort on the Western Front? (10 marks)

◆ *Use the source and recalled knowledge.*

SECTION 3

The Extended Essay

PLANNING THE EXTENDED ESSAY

What is the Extended Essay?

In Chapter 1 of this book, you learned how to write an essay. This section of the book will build on this skill for the Extended Essay. An Extended Essay is exactly what it says: a big essay.

But:

- ◆ **You** will choose the question that you will answer. (Your teacher will provide help if it is needed.)
- ◆ **You** will research the topic.
- ◆ **You** will write a plan of no more than 200 words to help you answer the question. You can take this into the write-up with you.
- ◆ **You** will write up the essay in a two-hour supervised session.

In other words, you will know the question, unlike when you sit the final examination for Paper 1. This means that the Extended Essay is an opportunity for you to show your essay-writing skills. It enables you to plan a response to the question well before the final write-up. This can be your best piece of work because you have the chance to work on it over a period of time. How that time is organised will depend on where you are studying. You will either work at the essay over a short, focused period of time, or you will complete it over a number of weeks.

How to choose a question

The question that you choose is very important. The course Arrangements say that you must choose an issue from within the periods that you are studying. So your question must come from the subjects that you are studying for Paper 1 or Paper 2. There are a number of things that you should be aware of when choosing a question.

The Extended Essay should be a piece of work that you enjoy doing. Therefore it is sensible to choose a subject area that you enjoy. If you enjoy the topic you are going to try harder. However, the topic must also be one that you can reasonably complete in the time you are given. It should be a mainstream topic where there are a lot of resources for you to look at.

Make sure that you are answering a proper question that requires you to assess a development or evaluate the reasons for a development/event. Your question must let you argue a point. It needs to let you debate before drawing an overall conclusion to the question.

Let us look at some examples. A question such as 'Why did Britain become democratic?' is not a good question because the answer will just be a list of the reasons why Britain became more democratic. A better question might be, 'To what extent did Britain become more democratic because of social and economic developments?' This is much better, because the question means that you must assess the importance of social and economic developments in the development of Britain as a democracy. This will mean that you will look at other factors such as the role of pressure groups as well. You will have to assess these other reasons before coming to an overall conclusion. A well-worded question can really help you.

A good starting point for a question is to look at the areas of the course that you have been studying for Paper 1. You can choose the issue for your Extended Essay from any part of this. An issue chosen from this area is likely to be on a mainstream topic that can be researched easily. If you are stuck, your teacher or lecturer should be able to help you. You can also create essays using topics from Paper 2. Although you do not get essay questions in Paper 2, the detailed description of the course content can be used to produce questions.

Key Points

◆   Make sure your essay is from a topic you study.

◆   Make sure your essay is on a topic you will enjoy studying.

◆   Make sure your essay question is well worded and allows you to argue a case.

◆   Make sure your essay is on a main topic that allows you to access a range of resources.

Planning your work

Although you will get time at school to study the Extended Essay, the more you manage to work at home the better your essay will be. This means that you will have to work independently. The teacher will give you deadlines, but how you achieve the work by that deadline is up to you. This means that you will need to plan your work.

First, you need to ensure that you have the resources to complete your essay successfully! You will already have the resources to start your work, but you will have to look for more sources.

For the Paper 1 essay, your notes and textbook give you what you need. They will not give you all that you need for a successful Extended Essay, but they will give you an excellent starting point. Use these resources as the framework to produce your overall plan. That means the outline areas you are going to include in the essay, along with some detail and argument.

For example, if you are researching an essay answering the question 'How important were the suffrage movements in women's achievement of the vote in 1918?', you may already know the reasons why women gained the vote in national elections in 1918. An awareness of the role of suffrage movements, the impact of the First World War, the example of other countries, and other developments for women before the war are what you might expect to use for a timed essay in an exam. They are also an excellent starting point for your Extended Essay. You already have a basic paragraph plan with this information.

You will now need to add detail and increase the sophistication of your argument. This means you will need to look at other sources of information. As part of the Higher History course, you learn to weigh up sources of evidence and comment on them. It is worthwhile doing this when looking for more information for your Extended Essay. Some material is very useful. Many schools and colleges have small departmental libraries as well as access to the institution library. Your teacher or lecturer will have chosen relevant and useful textbooks that can help.

Hints and Tips

Suppose you have found an academic history book on your subject, but it is very large and you do not have time to read all it. What do you do?

If you have an outline plan and know what is going to be in each paragraph, you can use the **index** to find out about specific topics. You can also get a real feel for the way a book is going to argue by reading the **introduction** and the **conclusion**. This is where authors will outline what they are going to do as well as summarise the arguments they have made. It is also where you can decide if it is worthwhile looking at the book in more depth.

Your teacher or lecturer may also have articles from journals, such as *History Today*, which can be very useful. Articles are helpful as they provide snapshots of research and are usually straightforward to understand. They may also have handy reading lists. Other sources are less useful. Be very careful if you use the Internet to research your Extended Essay. Some subjects that you may study are still controversial and there are websites out there whose authors have an 'agenda'. Such sites are very biased and should be avoided. On the other hand, some academic websites have articles that can be valuable. Do not download essays from any of the numerous sites that sell them. Your teacher will know your style and spot it if you do this.

HOW TO PASS HIGHER HISTORY

Key Points

◆ Use your existing textbooks and notes to create an outline topic plan for your essay. Use this information to decide on main topic areas you will need to discuss in your essay.

◆ Gather other relevant information for your essay from reliable sources such as your History department or institution library.

◆ Use articles and accessible books written by reputable historians.

◆ Take care when using the Internet to gather information. Use reputable websites to find information.

◆ In no circumstances cut and paste information direct from the Internet and pass it off as your own work.

What do you look for when reading other books and articles? The problems of note-taking!

Now you have found more textbooks and articles relevant to your essay, what do you do with them? You need to extract the relevant information for your essay.

You are looking for two things when you look at other information.

◆ More detail or examples to develop your argument.

◆ Views about the event you are studying. Historians have views and like to express them. These views are interpretations. An essay that shows an awareness of these interpretations generally gets more credit than one that does not.

These can be added to the outline plan you have worked out when doing the initial planning of the essay. You might have based this outline plan on a class essay you have done.

Hints and Tips

How you organise note-taking is up to you, but there are general points you should keep in mind.

◆ Where possible, use bullet points under general topic areas to summarise the paragraphs you have decided you are going to write about.

◆ Use your own words. Do not write out huge chunks of text from books. This is a waste of time and effort. Also, your teacher will know how you write. If you use work that someone else has created you will be caught.

◆ Look for key examples, arguments and information.

◆ If you find a good interpretation of the subject, write out short quotes that illustrate the interpretation. Even if you summarise views in your own words they can be used successfully in the Extended Essay.

◆ If you do use a historical viewpoint, make a note of the page where it is in the book or article in your notes. This will save time if you need to check back over the information.

Once you have gathered the information you need, you have to do something with it. It can be helpful to write out a brief outline of your essay – perhaps on a single sheet of paper. You can see where you have too much information and where you may need to do some more work. You will also get an idea of how long your essay will take to write. Remember, you will be writing up the essay in a two-hour supervised session in the school or college where you study, so using the time effectively is important. You should be ready to write for the full two hours.

How will I remember all this information?

Top tips for success – How to Plan!

As you know, 30 marks for Higher History are gained by completing the **Extended Essay**. This is completed before you sit the final exam so it is worthwhile spending time on it as these are marks you bank – in other words you have a basis for success even before the exam! It is in your interest to make sure you get the best mark possible. Since you are writing an Extended Essay, you are allowed to take a 200-word plan into the exam room where you will do your supervised two-hour write-up. One way of making sure you get the best mark possible for your Extended Essay is to make sure that your **essay plan** really helps you on the day of the write-up. A good essay plan directs you when writing your essay.

Your plan can help you in two main ways:

◆ **An aid to memory.** As you work on your Extended Essay you will identify many important facts and pieces of relevant information which you want to make use of in your Extended Essay. By including references to these facts in your plan, you are making sure **that you do not inadvertently leave out anything important** relating to the issue about which you are writing. This aspect of your plan is clearly a vital one – remember, you can earn up to **12 marks** for points of **knowledge and understanding** which are accurate and relevant.

However, remember that **it may not be a good idea** to write down **very** detailed facts in your plan. The best approach is probably to write **some** references to the key facts – just

enough to jog your memory, to act as a reminder. You **must** stick to the 200 word limit in your plan but there is **no limit** to what you can **remember**!

◆ **Organising and developing your Extended Essay.** A further **12 marks** can be earned for **argument and evaluation** – for how well you address the **issue** or **question** which you have set yourself in the title. As you prepare your plan, you should be thinking carefully about how your plan can assist you in doing this. You are not simply setting down facts and details but also, more importantly, you are setting down how you want **to make use of** this information.

For example, the issue or question may well deal with the **importance** or **significance** of something, probably in relation to other factors. It would be an excellent idea to include some of your ideas on this information in your plan. It is more likely to help you to keep a clear focus on the issue or question, and this should help you to increase your score on the **12 marks** available for argument and evaluation.

There are also things that you should not do:

◆ Don't run over the 200-word limit. Marks will be taken off if you do!

◆ Don't use symbols that mean something to you, but cannot be understood by a marker. Again, you will have marks taken off if you do this.

◆ Don't cross out words on the plan. It should be neat and tidy and easy to read. Word-processing your plan is a good idea!

◆ Don't write out huge chunks of information using conjunctions like 'and' or 'but'. You will be wasting words if you do.

What You Should Know

What counts as a word in your 200-word plan? A word is not just a written word; it can also be a date, a number or a recognised historical abbreviation like NUWSS or WSPU. It is easier to shorten the National Union of Women's Suffrage Society to NUWSS. This is a well-known organisation, so using the term NUWSS is allowed and counts as one word. **Only** use well-known abbreviations like this. If you decide to make one up, you will have marks taken off.

Remember

Your plan is a way of remembering key information, and even arguments, too. Keep it simple and easy to understand. Both you and the person who marks your essay will appreciate this.

Let's look at an example of an Extended Essay title and, more importantly, how the plan could be presented.

Here is the title:

'How important was the role of the suffrage organisations in the decision to grant the right to vote to the majority of women in 1918?'

As a title for an Extended Essay, this is perfectly acceptable. It is very definitely an issue or question – the importance of the suffrage organisations in the decision to grant the right to vote to the majority of women in 1918.

Now, let's suppose that this is the title of **your** Extended Essay. A number of things need to be done in order to succeed in this Extended Essay. You will need to think carefully and you will need to plan it carefully.

Assignment

Write down the title of the essay on a sheet of paper.

Now, write out a brief outline of how you think you would tackle this essay. You can use bullet points if you like.

This brief outline is, of course, the beginnings of a potential plan.

Think about the facts you might want to use.

Now, think about how you might develop your arguments.

You are now going to look at two versions of possible plans for this Extended Essay. For each plan, your task will be to produce a **commentary** on it.

You should:

◆   Identify the **strengths** of the plans.

◆   Identify any **weaknesses** or **omissions**.

◆   Write down the **facts** in the plans.

◆   Write down any points of **argument and evaluation** which are being used.

◆   Decide which of the two plans is more likely to help you to produce an **effective and successful Extended Essay**.

Version 1

'How important was the role of the suffrage organisations in the decision to grant the right to vote to the majority of women in 1918?'

Introduction	Women's suffrage campaigns – NUWSS and WSPU – used different methods Votes at age 30 – 1918
Suffrage organisations	WSPU – leaders, Emmeline Pankhurst and daughters Christabel and Sylvia 'Deeds not Words' – militant – disrupting political meetings, vandalism and arson – Emily Davison, 1913 Derby Arrests – hunger-striking – force-feeding – cruel and dangerous Cat and Mouse Act – release and then arrest again NUWSS – led by Millicent Fawcett – held meetings, wrote letters to newspapers, marches, posters Non-violent – large membership and support – branches all over Britain Meetings with MPs
Reform Acts	Second Reform Act 1867 – male householders in the boroughs and also male lodgers who paid rent of £10 a year or more – reduced property threshold in the counties and gave the vote to agricultural workers
Other factors	Suffrage movements were important – but not as important as other factors in getting women the vote in 1918, such as the hundreds of thousands who worked in munitions during World War One
The Vote	Representation of the People Act 1918 – votes for all men at 21 Votes for women householders or wives of householders at 30
Conclusion	The Suffrage organisations helped them to win the vote in 1918 – also, other factors such as war work

194 words

Version 2

'How important was the role of the suffrage organisations in the decision to grant the right to vote to the majority of women in 1918?'

Introduction	Suffrage organisations – NUWSS, WSPU – activity up to 1914 Other factors – war work before 1914 – changing attitudes – views of politicians
Suffrage organisations	NUWSS – Mrs. Fawcett – NUWSS – non-violent **Importance** – built up support – membership Labour MPs, many Liberal MPs backed votes for women WSPU – Pankhursts – 'Deeds not Words' – Pankhursts – militant campaign – **examples** **Importance** – very successful – generated publicity – newspapers Negative publicity – 'wild' campaign – **examples** Loss of public support, 1911–14 – 'Cause marching backwards'

War Work	Industry – munitions factories, transport, Land Army (food production) – armed forces – nurses **Importance** – affected attitudes – women's contribution to war – **vital** Work seen as important in victory Women proved their value to the country WSPU campaign called off – Pankhursts backed war effort – responsible **Important** – affected attitudes – positive view of women
Democracy?	War for democracy? **Important** – view of war – vote to all men over 21 – exclude women? Example of New Zealand
Gratitude?	**Important** – factor – government **was** grateful to women Total support during war
Self-Interest?	1918 – Votes for Women – a popular move? **Important point** – country would support New women voters – likely to support Lloyd George in election
Conclusion	Suffrage organisations – publicity and support – some negative Other factors – war work, democracy, attitudes, self-interest

190 Words

Version 1

Well, what did you think of Version 1 of the plan for the Extended Essay?

It certainly has some **reasonable points**.

◆ The candidate has recognised the need for a definite **introduction** and a **conclusion**.

◆ The candidate has made use of **acceptable** abbreviations – ones which are in standard use (NUWSS, WSPU) – and which are counted as single words in the plan.

◆ The candidate has written some **headings**, although the relevance of some of these is perhaps not clear.

◆ **There is some relevant and accurate information** – points of knowledge and understanding.

However, it is fairly clear that this plan has a number of **weaknesses**.

◆ Some areas that might be considered important, such as the changing attitudes of powerful politicians or the concept of a war for democracy are **simply not mentioned**.

◆ **The candidate wastes a substantial quantity of words**. Look at how frequently words such as 'the', 'in', and 'as' are used. These words could easily have been omitted, thereby freeing up space for relevant knowledge, and points of analysis.

◆ More seriously, there is no indication at all in the plan of how the candidate intends to **use** the information which has been assembled, nor is it clear how the candidate intends to tackle the issue in the Extended Essay title.

◆ This plan is basically **a limited collection of facts** relevant to the issue (in some cases, of fairly marginal relevance) – and that is all that it is. The candidate would have been better to give some thought as to how this information could be organised and used to address the issue.

Version 2

The second version of the plan has some significant differences.

It has some very clear **strengths**.

◆ In the introduction, the candidate has identified **the need to place the issue in context**, recognising that the role of the suffrage organisations was linked to women gaining the vote, along with a number of other factors.

◆ In the conclusion, the candidate again recognises the need to **make an overall answer** to the question being posed, by linking the issue of the suffrage organisations to the other factors.

◆ **There are clear headings**, setting out sections of the Extended Essay, and the factors to be covered – the suffrage organisations and their campaigns and also other factors such as war work, war for democracy, the question of gratitude, and political self-interest. All of the headings are relevant to the issue.

◆ As the plan proceeds, it is very obvious that this candidate is determined to maintain a very definite focus on the issue. Look at how often in the plan the words **importance** and **important** are used – echoing and repeating the same word from the title. This candidate understands that he or she must try to **use** their information and knowledge to address the issue and has constructed and devised a plan which will help in this!

Does the plan have any **weaknesses**?

◆ The obvious point is that, compared to the previous example, this plan has **less factual content** and this could be considered to be a weakness.

◆ However, if this is a weakness, it may not be a serious one. After all, there is no limit to how much you can remember!

◆ In the second plan, it looks like the candidate has made a conscious decision to use more of the 200-word allocation to help keep a clear and definite focus on the issue. In the second plan, the candidate is relying more on **memory** to earn the 12 marks which are available for clear and relevant points of **knowledge and understanding**. However, the plan is structured very clearly to support the candidate in gaining a good score from the further 12 marks which are available for **argument and evaluation**.

Should I refer to historians in my Extended Essay?

This is a subject which often comes up when candidates are preparing their Extended Essays.

The Extended Essay is a major piece of work, on which you will spend a substantial amount of time and effort: you need to work hard if you want to get as good a mark as possible and you need to understand the significance of the Extended Essay.

As you work, you will read as widely as possible, as directed by your teacher. You will certainly begin with class notes and then, perhaps, look at books or more probably extracts from books, written by **historians**! So now you can add to your notes on your chosen issue some comments and statements by **real** historians – individuals who have studied the topic in considerable depth.

So … what about quoting from some of these historians in your Extended Essay? Is this going to get you a better mark?

Let's go back to something we looked at earlier and remind ourselves of the real basics of writing a good Extended Essay – the need to keep a **clear focus** on the issue.

As you know, **12 marks** are available for argument and evaluation – for how well you address the issue of your Extended Essay. In other words, for how well you answer the question! Hopefully, by now, you understand the importance of this. If you are considering including a quotation from a historian, ask yourself why you want to do this. Are you simply trying to show to the examiner that you have looked at something written by a historian? This could be a **bad move**!

Remember that the marker is looking for clear evidence that you are focusing on an issue, that you are addressing the specific question in the essay title. Quotations from historians which are simply there for their own sake, and may be unrelated to the issue, are not going to achieve anything. They may even **cost** you marks by reducing the extent to which you address the issue!

Recognising debate and differing opinions

Your ability to do this will depend on how much and how extensively you read and understand. Historians frequently hold differing views and will emphasise different aspects of a problem or issue. They may disagree!

For example, historians certainly hold a range of opinions on many issues including the effectiveness of the Liberal Government, 1906–1914, or the importance of the various factors leading to the Unification of Germany. If you **understand** some of the different points of view and debate, and **how they relate to your chosen issue**, then well done! You have probably got a pretty thorough grasp of your topic. By all means, go right ahead and make use of this information, so long as it is clearly related to your subject. If you can do this successfully and demonstrate that you have some **awareness** of varying opinions, then that, for Higher level, is probably sufficient. There is no need or requirement to make use of quotations from historians.

WRITING YOUR EXTENDED ESSAY

Let's start with two simple but very important points:

1. The Extended Essay is awarded marks out of 30 – and that means 30% of your overall mark for Higher History.

So your Extended Essay is important.

What You Should Know

A successful Extended Essay gives you a big advantage as you prepare for the final exam. If you have written an Extended Essay which is clear, well-presented and well-structured, you will almost certainly have gained quite a substantial block of marks. As you start the final exam, this should be a boost to your confidence – you hit the ground running!

2. The Extended Essay is … an essay.

It will have to be longer and contain more detailed information and more developed analysis than the essays which you have been working on for Paper 1. But the Extended Essay is basically done in the same way.

Key Points

The Extended Essay will have:

◆   an introduction
◆   a development
◆   a conclusion.

So let's start by revisiting each of these three vital areas, to remind ourselves of what we need to do.

Introduction

In the introduction, we are introducing the subject – the issue we are dealing with – to the reader. In this case, the reader is the person who is going to mark your Extended Essay.

Just as with the essays for Paper 1, there are a number of things which you should be trying to do in your introduction.

◆   Make it clear that you have **understood** the issue, and that you have a very clear focus on it.
◆   Attempt to set the issue in its **wider context** – demonstrate that you have an awareness of the **background** of the issue you are dealing with.

- Make some kind of indication to the reader of your likely **approach** to the question – set out briefly how you intend to tackle it.
- Hold the reader's attention!

Development

The development is the central section of your Extended Essay, and is certainly the longest and most substantial section. You should gain most of your marks here.

You have **two** clear priorities here. The first is to demonstrate and prove your **knowledge** and **understanding** of the issue you are writing about. You must make it clear and obvious to the marker that you know and understand the main facts and relevant knowledge. You should not omit any important information, nor should you include anything which is irrelevant to your chosen issue. From the knowledge and information which you are deploying, it should be obvious to the marker that **you know your subject**. You have done your reading and research effectively – you know and understand the key facts.

The second important thing that you have to do is to demonstrate that you are able to make use of the skills which are necessary in writing an effective History essay – that you can **analyse** and **evaluate**, **argue a case** where required and make **judgements**.

You do this in exactly the same way as you have learned in tackling the essay questions in Paper 1 – that is, by doing what the question is asking you to do. There is, of course, a difference in the Extended Essay: this time, **you** made up the question!

If, for example, the title of the essay asks you to make a judgement about something, that is exactly what you are going to do. Again, if the title asks you to consider the importance of an isolated factor in causing something, you will begin by looking at the isolated factor, before moving on to consider other factors.

In this way, by doing what the question is asking you to do (that really means doing what you have asked yourself to do!), you will effectively be using the skills of analysis, evaluation, arguing a case and making judgements. The marker will recognise this, and reward you appropriately.

Conclusion

Finally, you must bring your essay to a conclusion – you must write an overall answer to the question in the title. Just as with Paper 1, the conclusion is a vital part of the essay. You are addressing the issue which you set yourself at the start, in the introduction.

So how do you write an effective conclusion? Well, an effective conclusion will have to do several things:

◆ It will develop, fairly naturally, from the points which you have made in the development section, summing up your findings and views.

◆ It should be a balanced conclusion, revisiting, fairly briefly, the points of evaluation, judgement and analysis which you have made in the development.

◆ It should provide, as clearly as possible, an overall answer to the question that you set yourself.

Key Points

As you start to write your Extended Essay, you have a number of things going for you.

◆ You chose the subject and the issue to study.

◆ You have spent time working on your Extended Essay, both in class and elsewhere. You have made use of a number of resources to support your study – you will certainly have used your class notes and textbooks, and you will have read a bit more widely than this, under the guidance of your teacher, using library resources.

◆ By now, you know this subject pretty thoroughly!

◆ You will be given quite a substantial amount of time to write your Extended Essay – two hours.

◆ Above all, you have your plan beside you as you write, so you are not going to forget anything important! Your plan will prompt you on the key points of knowledge that you wish to include. And it should do more than this – your plan should help you to organise your thoughts and ideas, and help you to make use of the facts and knowledge which you have gathered.

Knowledge and understanding

In your Extended Essay you should be able to write in a bit more detail than in a Paper 1 type of essay. There are a couple of fairly obvious reasons why this should be possible.

You will have spent roughly two weeks working on your Extended Essay before you begin writing it. You should have made good use of the time available – reading and annotating your class notes, reading more widely from the school and local libraries, using Internet resources – gathering quite a substantial body of relevant information. By the end of this period of preparation, you should know the subject quite well. You will be in command of a substantial body of knowledge – you will know the key facts.

Also, you have your plan beside you as you write your Extended Essay. The plan, with its allowance of up to 200 words, will undoubtedly help you to remember essential points of knowledge and understanding. In fact, one of the most effective ways to use the plan is as an aid to your memory! The plan must stay within the 200-word limit, but there is no limit on how much you can remember!

What You Should Know

Twelve marks are awarded for points of **knowledge** and **understanding**. A mark is awarded for each relevant point of knowledge introduced. It is also possible that, if a point of knowledge is developed further, it may be worthy of a second mark.

So if your Extended Essay shows that you have studied your chosen subject carefully, and that you really know it, you can expect to be rewarded in terms of marks.

Your Extended Essay is part of the Higher History course, and at this level you are expected to have a greater command of knowledge, along with the ability to write in a bit more detail, than in exams you have done previously.

Perhaps a few examples might be helpful, to give at least an idea of the level of writing that is expected.

Subject	Unlikely to be worth a mark	Knowledge/understanding points possibly worth a mark
Reign of David I of Scotland	David I developed the royal system of justice.	David I developed the royal system of justice to include the use of juries and sheriffs acting in the name of the king.
Career of William Wallace	Wallace defeated an English army at the battle of Stirling Bridge.	Wallace won an important victory at the battle of Stirling Bridge in 1297, where his much smaller army outwitted and defeated a powerful and well-equipped English force commanded by the Earl of Surrey.
Reign of Mary, Queen of Scots	Mary faced many problems from the powerful Scottish nobility.	Mary faced many problems from the powerful Scottish nobility, who were often very hostile to her. At the start of her reign, she had to deal with a revolt by the powerful Earl of Huntly.
The Liberal Reforms	The Liberal Government introduced Old Age Pensions.	The Liberal Government of 1906–1914 introduced the Old Age Pension Act, which provided pensions for British people when they reached the age of 70.
The Labour Government	The Labour Government introduced the National Health Service.	The Labour Government worked to improve the health of the British people by introducing the National Health Service, which was to be universal, comprehensive and free at the point of treatment.

In other words, simply mentioning a point of knowledge or understanding may not be enough in itself to earn a mark. You need to give some detail, to demonstrate that you really understand your subject.

You should include as much relevant knowledge in your Extended Essay as possible. As long as this knowledge and understanding is relevant and accurate, and demonstrates some understanding of the topic, you will gain marks on the knowledge and understanding scale. There is no need to stop once you have written twelve points!

If you have fairly extensive knowledge and understanding – if you really know your stuff – you could get the maximum marks for knowledge and understanding, a full twelve marks.

What You Should Know

Suppose your essay is well stocked with relevant and accurate knowledge and understanding – in fact, it is positively overflowing with knowledge and understanding. Congratulations! You have obtained the maximum marks for knowledge and understanding, and there is quite a bit to spare.

Does this mean that this 'extra' knowledge and understanding is wasted?

No! You can't analyse or evaluate in a vacuum. Your knowledge and understanding, including those parts of it which are 'overflowing' or 'extra', are vital in the second scale of marks used in the Extended Essay – the twelve marks which are available for **analysis** and **evaluation**.

In Higher History, whether in the Extended Essay or in Paper 1, you must use the skills of analysis and evaluation. This means answering the question and addressing the issue. You can only do this with accurate, detailed and relevant knowledge and understanding. So the more of this there is the better.

Analysis and evaluation

Just as in the essays that you have been working on for Paper 1, you need to demonstrate your skills of analysis and evaluation in the Extended Essay. Here of course you have a bit more time to do the analysing and evaluating – a full two hours. So it is worth making this your very best effort.

What You Should Know

Twelve marks are allocated for analysis and evaluation – that is twelve of the 30 marks for the Extended Essay. So it is really important that you try to attain as high a mark as possible, that you maximise your marks.

Remember

A T Q

ANSWER THE QUESTION!

Do what the question is asking you to do, just as you have been learning to do with your answers to Paper 1 questions. If you do this, you are almost certainly developing the skills of analysis and evaluation.

In your Extended Essay you do have a slight edge – you made up the question, and you have spent a couple of weeks working on it. You will almost certainly have spent some of this time

thinking about your question. This thinking time is developing your skills of analysis and evaluation.

Perhaps you would like a little reminder about analysis and evaluation? Of course you would!

Let's say that the question you have devised asks you to consider the importance of a single, isolated factor in causing something. You begin by explaining the importance of the factor – the reasons for its significance – and go into some detail. As you work through your explanation, you are certainly making use of factual knowledge, but you are also analysing and evaluating.

You now proceed to examine other factors linked to the same issue, explaining and demonstrating how important you think they are in relation to the issue. Once more, you are analysing and evaluating.

Your question requires you to make some form of judgement about something – to examine a significant development or trend, and to explain how far it progressed. Once again, as you use your factual knowledge to give this explanation, you are analysing and evaluating.

Here are some possible Extended Essay questions.

Example

In each example, try to work out **what the question is asking you to do** – outline briefly the **analysis** and **evaluation** you would need to carry out if this was your Extended Essay question.

- To what extent did David I succeed in developing the power of the monarchy in Scotland?
- To what extent was Robert Bruce more interested in his own gain than in Scottish independence?
- How important was the desire for protection in the development of towns in England and Scotland?
- To what extent was the decline of serfdom due to the onset of the Black Death in the fourteenth century?
- To what extent was the Reformation of 1560 brought about by the weaknesses of the Roman Catholic Church in Scotland?
- To what extent was Charles I's dispute with Parliament due to financial problems?
- To what extent did Scotland benefit from the experience of migration and the Empire, up to 1939?
- To what extent was the crisis in Scottish identity the most important impact of the Great War?
- How important were concerns about national efficiency in leading the Liberal Government of 1906–14 to introduce social reforms?
- To what extent had Britain become a democracy by 1918?
- How important was Prussian military strength in the achievement of German unification by 1870?
- To what extent were the increased powers of the federal government, as developed during the New Deal, effective in dealing with the problems facing the American people during the 1930s?

How much analysis and evaluation should you write?

You have two hours to complete your Extended Essay, and there are up to twelve marks available for analysis and evaluation. Obviously, then, you are going to try hard to include as much analysis and evaluation as you can – you will try to write in an analytical and evaluative style.

Twelve marks are available for analysis and evaluation. How do you move your mark as far as possible up the scale from zero to twelve?

◆ Quantity – **how much** analysis and evaluation is written.

◆ Quality – **how successful** the analysis and evaluation is.

Hints and Tips

Some characteristics of analysis and evaluation:

◆ **Sometimes fairly thin.** In some Extended Essays, the analysis and evaluation are rather thin and slight, with perhaps an occasional sentence here and there, only barely addressing the issue. Not surprisingly, this approach is almost certainly going to stay at the lower end of the mark scale.

◆ **A bit more focused.** Here the candidate is trying hard to address the issue in the question. The style of the essay may be rather descriptive but at least there are some short comments, rather than the occasional isolated sentence.

◆ **An awareness of the issue.** In many Extended Essays, candidates show a fairly clear and consistent awareness of the issue they are tackling. Accurate and relevant knowledge is deployed, as well as developed analysis and evaluation of these knowledge points, showing a definite understanding of the issue being considered. This awareness of the issue is recognised by further progress on the mark scale.

◆ **Sustained analysis and evaluation.** Here the candidate demonstrates a very clear understanding of the issue, and makes very effective use of factual knowledge to support and reinforce the arguments being presented. Extended Essays of this style are effectively being driven and directed by analysis and evaluation and, for this reason, are likely to score at the upper end of the mark scale.

Structure

The final six marks are awarded for structure – for how effectively your Extended Essay is organised. Structure marks are attained from the three main components of the essay – the introduction, the development and the conclusion.

The introduction

What is meant by an **effective** introduction? First of all, think about how well the subject or issue of the Extended Essay has been introduced to the reader. This is the key reason for having an introduction.

For example, is the introduction very brief, perhaps only consisting of a single sentence? This would certainly act as an introduction, but is not likely to be doing much to help the reader to understand what the essay is about. What is more effective is to try to develop the introduction a little. Ask yourself, does the introduction attempt to set the issue in its wider context, as you have learned to do while working on essays for Paper 1? Does the introduction make an attempt to outline some of the background to the chosen issue?

Then, continuing with the idea of introducing the subject of the essay to the reader, does the introduction set out, briefly but clearly, the likely approach to be taken? Does it make clear how you are going to tackle the subject?

Clearly, if you try to organise your introduction in this manner, you are more likely to gain marks on the structure scale.

The development

The development of the Extended Essay, just as in the essays for Paper 1, is the most extensive section of your work. It is where you will deploy your knowledge and understanding, and your analysis and evaluation – and, obviously, where you hope to gain a substantial number of marks.

However, you can also gain marks in this section for structure, for how your development is arranged and organised. For example, is your development section organised clearly and logically? Is it set out in a straightforward manner and basically easy to follow? Or is it a bit disorganised and haphazard?

Above all, the development section should always keep a clear focus on the question, on the issue being addressed in the Extended Essay. It is very good practice to make clear to the reader that you are keeping the question in mind throughout the essay. An effective way to do this is to keep referring, briefly, to the question as you work through the development. You can do this by means of linking sentences, often quite short, in which you remind yourself, and the reader, of the issue which you are dealing with.

The conclusion

Finally, you need to give some thought to how to bring your Extended Essay to as effective a conclusion as possible. Remember, you have two weeks to prepare for writing your Extended Essay, so some of that time, probably towards the end of the preparation, can be devoted to planning an effective conclusion.

What makes a conclusion effective?

As you have been working through the development of your essay, you have been trying to keep a clear focus on the question which you set yourself in the title. Now, in the conclusion, you are going to make an **overall** answer to that question – based on the evidence, the knowledge and

Remember

Think back to a hint earlier in this chapter: **A T Q** – Answer The Question!

understanding, and the analysis and evaluation which you have been presenting as you worked through the essay.

By this time, if your efforts have been successful, it should be becoming clear to the reader where your essay is going. In the conclusion, you are now going to sum up, and pull all your evidence and arguments together, to reach a decision about the question.

So, if the question asked you to consider the significance of an isolated factor in causing something, in your conclusion you are going to address its significance – you are going to state clearly and concisely **how significant you believe it to have been**. If the question asked you to make a judgement about how far a development or trend had progressed, you are going to **make that judgement**.

The key point is that you are going to write this conclusion based on what you have already written in your development. In the development you looked at a series of points or factors in turn, dealing with them one at a time. Now you are simply pulling them all together, and trying to write a clear overall conclusion to your Extended Essay. You are reminding yourself and the reader that, throughout your essay, you have been addressing a clear and well-defined issue. From the work which you have done in the development, you can now, with some confidence, bring the essay to an end.

If you can try to do this, you have an excellent chance of writing an **effective** conclusion, which will be recognised with marks on the structure scale.

Summary

Your Extended Essay is – an essay! It should be more substantial and detailed than standard class essays, written as practice for Paper 1, but it remains an essay. However, it is a very important essay, in terms of the marks awarded and its impact on your overall grade in Higher History.

If you focus clearly on the points made in this chapter, on the need for clear and careful planning and organisation, and on the significance of each of the three sections – the introduction, the development and the conclusion – you will be prepared for the completion of an effective and successful Extended Essay.

Best of luck!

APPENDIX

The Wars of Independence

1 Scotland 1286–96: The Succession Problem and the Great Cause

How fully…the succession problem in Scotland, 1286–92?

Detailed content:

The succession problem; the Guardians; the Treaty of Birgham; the death of the Maid of Norway; the Scottish appeal to Edward I – the decision at Norham; Bruce versus Balliol; the Great Cause and Edward's decision.

How far…the problems caused by the death of Alexander III?
How far…the reasons for the Scots' appeal to Edward?
How far…Edward's resolution of the Great Cause?

2 John Balliol and Edward I

How fully…the relationship between John Balliol and Edward I?

Detailed content:

Balliol's rule; Edward's overlordship; the Scottish response; the Anglo–French war and the Franco–Scottish Treaty; the subjugation of Scotland.

How far…John Balliol's difficulties in ruling Scotland?
How far…Scottish responses to Edward's overlordship?
How far…Edward's subjugation of the Scots in 1296?

3 William Wallace and Scottish resistance

How fully…Scottish resistance to Edward I, 1296–1305?

Detailed content:

Scottish resistance; roles of William Wallace and Andrew Murray; victory at Stirling and its effects on Scots and on Scotland; defeat at Falkirk and continuing Scottish resistance.

How far…the growth of Scottish resistance to Edward I, 1296–7?
How far…the changing military balance between Scotland and England, 1298–1301?
How far…the crushing of Scottish resistance by Edward, 1301–05?

4 The rise and triumph of Robert Bruce

How fully…the reasons for the ultimate success of Bruce in maintaining Scotland's independence?

Detailed content:

The ambitions of Robert Bruce; his conflict with and victory over Scottish opponents; his victory at Bannockburn; continuing hostilities; the Declaration of Arbroath; the Treaties of Edinburgh/Northampton, 1328.

How far...the opposition of many Scots to Robert Bruce?
How far...Robert Bruce's abilities as a military leader?
How far...the methods used by Bruce to attain the peace settlement made with England in 1328?

The Age of Reformation

1 The Reformation of 1560

How fully...the reasons for the Reformation of 1560?

Detailed content:

The nature of the Church in Scotland; attempts at reform; the growth of Protestantism; relationships with France and England; religious conflict; Lords of the Congregation; Treaty of Edinburgh, 1560.

How far...the weaknesses of the Catholic Church in Scotland?
How far...the growth of Protestantism?
How far...the influence of England and/or France on religious developments in Scotland?

2 The reign of Mary, 1561–1567

How fully...the reasons for Mary's loss of her throne?

Detailed content:

Mary's difficulties in ruling Scotland: religion; gender; relations with the nobility; Mary's marriages; her relationship with England; abdication; flight to England.

How far...Mary's difficulties in ruling Scotland?
How far...Mary's relationship with England?
How far...the contribution Mary, Queen of Scots, made to the loss of her throne?

3 James VI and the relationship between monarch and Kirk

How fully...the relationship between Monarch and Kirk in the reign of James VI?

Detailed content:

The struggle for control of the Kirk: from regency to personal rule; differing views about the roles of the monarch and Kirk.

How far...the efforts of James VI to control the Kirk?
How far...the efforts of the Kirk to maintain its independence?
How far...the outcome of the attempts of James VI to control the Kirk by 1603?

4 The impact of the Reformation on Scotland, to 1603

How fully...the impact of the Reformation on Scotland?

The social, cultural, educational and economic impact of the Reformation on Scotland, to 1603.

How far...the social impact of the Reformation on Scotland, to 1603?
How far...the cultural impact of the Reformation on Scotland, to 1603?
How far...the economic impact of the Reformation on Scotland, to 1603?

The Treaty of Union

1 Worsening relations with England

How fully...the reasons for worsening relations with England?

Detailed content:

Navigation Acts; England's foreign wars; Scotland's economic problems; famine; Darien Scheme and its failure; Scottish responses; incidents leading to worsening relations with England; the War of the Spanish Succession; the issue of the succession.

How far...the economic problems faced by Scotland?
How far...the relationship between the Scottish Parliament and England?
How far...the problems arising from a shared monarchy?

2 Arguments for and against union with England

How fully...the arguments for and against a union with England?

Detailed content:

Religious issues; the Scottish economy: possible advantages of Scots having access to English colonies; the issue of Scottish identity; contrasting attitudes in Scotland towards Union.

How far...arguments for union with England?
How far...arguments against union with England?
How far...attitudes towards union in Scotland?

3 The passing of the Act of Union

How fully...the reasons for the passing of the Treaty of Union?

Detailed content:

The changing attitude of England; the debate over a Federal or Incorporating Union; the role of the Commissioners; negotiations; the passing of the Union by the Scottish Parliament.

How far...English attitudes towards union?
How far...debate over a Federal or Incorporating Union?
How far...the passage of the Union through the Scottish Parliament?

4 The effects of the Union, to 1740

How fully…the effects of the Union, up to 1740?

Detailed content:

Economic effects, to 1740: agriculture, manufacture and trade; political effects; the Hanoverian succession and the causes of the Jacobite Rising of 1715.

How far…economic effects of the Union, to 1740?
How far…political effects of the Union, to 1740?
How far…the causes of the Jacobite Rising of 1715?

Migration and Empire

1 The migration of Scots

How fully…the reasons for the migration of Scots?

Detailed content:

Push and pull factors in internal migration and emigration: economic. social, cultural and political aspects; opportunity and coercion.

How far…the reasons for internal migration within Scotland?
How far…the opportunities that attracted Scots to other lands?
How far…the factors that forced Scots to leave Scotland?

2 The experience of immigrants in Scotland

How fully…the experience of immigrants in Scotland?

Detailed content:

The experience of immigrants, with reference to Catholic Irish, Protestant Irish, Jews, Lithuanians and Italians; the reactions of Scots to immigrants; issues of identity and assimilation.

How far…the social and economic conditions experienced by immigrants to Scotland?
How far…relations between native Scots and immigrants?
How far…the assimilation of immigrants into Scottish society?

3 The impact of Scots emigrants on the Empire

How fully…the impact of Scots emigrants* on the Empire?

Detailed content:

The impact of Scots emigrants on the growth and development of the Empire with reference to Canada, Australia, New Zealand and India in terms of: Economy and enterprise; Culture and religion; Native societies.

How far…the contribution of Scots to the economic growth and development of the Empire?
How far…the contribution of Scots to the religious and cultural development of the Empire?
How far…the impact of the activities of Scots emigrants* on native societies in the Empire?

*For this purpose emigrants will be taken to include Scots involved in government in India.

4 The effects of migration and the Empire on Scotland, to 1939

How fully…the effects of migration and the Empire on Scotland?

Detailed content:

The contribution of immigrants to Scottish society, economy and culture; the impact of the Empire on Scotland.

How far…the social and cultural impact of immigrants on Scotland?
How far…the economic contribution of immigrants to Scotland?
How far…the importance of the Empire to Scotland's development?

The Impact of the Great War

1 Scots on the Western Front

How fully…the involvement of Scots on the Western Front?

Detailed content:

Voluntary recruitment; the experience of Scots on the Western Front, with reference to the battles of Loos and the Somme; the kilted regiments; the role of Scottish military personnel in terms of commitment, casualties, leadership and overall contribution to the military effort.

How far…the reasons why so many Scots volunteered to fight in the Great War?
How far…the experience of Scots on the Western Front?
How far…the contribution of Scots to the military effort on the Western Front?

2 Domestic impact of war: society and culture

How fully…the impact of the war on Scottish society?

Detailed content:

Recruitment and conscription; pacifism and conscientious objection; DORA; changing role of women in wartime, including rent strikes; scale and effects of military losses on Scottish society; commemoration and remembrance.

How far…the issues in the debate over conscription?
How far…the impact of the war on Scottish women?
How far…the impact of military losses on Scottish society?

3 Domestic impact of war: industry and economy

How fully…the impact of the war on the Scottish economy, 1914–1928?

Detailed content:

Wartime effects of war on industry, agriculture and fishing; price rises and rationing; post-war economic change and difficulties; post-war emigration; the land issue in the Highlands and Islands.

How far…the effects of the war on the Scottish economy up to 1918?
How far…the economic difficulties faced by Scotland after 1918?
How far…the reasons so many Scots left Scotland after 1918?

4 Domestic impact of war: politics

How fully...the impact of the war on political developments in Scotland?

Detailed content:

The impact of the war on political developments as exemplified by the growth of radicalism, the ILP and Red Clydeside, continuing support for political unionism and the crisis of Scottish identity.

How far...the growth of radicalism in politics in Scotland?
How far...the strength of support in Scotland for the Union?
How far...the crisis in Scottish identity that developed after 1918?